D0342268

Outposts of Eden

Books by Page Stegner

To My Father

The Sierra Club, founded in 1892 by John Muir, has devoted itself to the study and protection of the earth's scenic and ecological resources—mountains, wetlands, woodlands, wild shores and rivers, deserts and plains. The publishing program of the Sierra Club offers books to the public as a nonprofit educational service in the hope that they may enlarge the public's understanding of the Club's basic concerns. The point of view expressed in each book, however, does not necessarily represent that of the Club. The Sierra Club has some sixty chapters coast to coast, in Canada, Hawaii, and Alaska. For information about how you may participate in its programs to preserve wilderness and the quality of life, please address inquiries to Sierra Club, 730 Polk Street, San Francisco, CA 94109.

Library of Congress Cataloging-in-Publication Data

Stegner, Page.
  Outposts of Eden / Page Stegner.
    p. cm.
  ISBN 0-87156-672-9
    1. Nature conservation—West (U.S.) 2. Environmental protection—West (U.S.) 3. West (U.S.)—Description and travel. I. Title.
QH76.5.W34S74 1989
333.78'16'0978—dc 19   88-26320
                                                     CIP

Production by Eileen Max
Jacket design by Paul Bacon
Book design by Seventeenth Street Studios
Printed in the United States of America

10 9 8 7 6 5 4 3 2 1

Outposts of Eden

A CURMUDGEON AT LARGE
IN THE AMERICAN WEST

Page Stegner

Sierra Club Books · *San Francisco*

Contents

Introduction

*I*T HAS TAKEN ME nearly fifty years to find out where I belong, though I got the first serious message in 1973 when I returned to the United States after several years of Peace Corps duty in Ecuador and Venezuela. It took a while to hear the voices, but when I did they came in loud and clear. Very loud and clear.

I remember snow on the ground in Washington as I went about turning in my diplomatic passport, filing my mustering-out papers, saying farewell to some of the D.C. staff. The trees were black and leafless. An icy wind cut through my semitropical suit and lightweight raincoat whenever I left the overheated government buildings and walked the few blocks to my hotel to kill time before the next appointment, the next lunch, breakfast, dinner, the next invitation. Any invitation. I had a teaching job waiting in California but the term didn't start for nearly a month, and while I had friends in Washington and thought I was in no rush to return to the West Coast, it was not a particularly jolly time. I had the end-of-something blues, perhaps.

The only real decision I had to make was whether to

fly home or take a train to Vermont and get the car I had left at my parents' summer house and drive it to California. I chose the latter to give myself time "to think about the future." It took a day or two getting the car in shape, and then, still dallying, still courting invitations, I called my former editor at the Dial Press, Bill Decker, and said I'd be coming through New York City on my way west. Generous man, he managed to sound pleased and invited me to dinner. "I'll be there tomorrow afternoon between five and seven," I told him.

It snowed some more on the way down from Vermont. The woods bordering the turnpike were grey and dismal, and a dense fog enveloped the roadway all the way across Massachusetts. By the time I reached Connecticut I was starting to sweat, and not from heat. The Merritt Parkway was a speed freak's nightmare, an LP world played at 78, zero visibility, negative control, bumper to bumper, rocker panel to rocker panel, everyone locked in place next to a concrete wall with the radio blaring and the hammer down. The high-pitched whine I thought I heard coming from the transmission turned out to be me.

By the time I found myself in Manhattan and driving south on Amsterdam past 109th Street (where in 1958 I had an apartment with a guy named Larry Morris), I was totally convinced I was the victim of a diabolical time warp. I dream about it still. Buildings lean in on me, blotting out the twilight sky; stunt men in golf caps commit unspeakable maneuvers with taxi cabs and buses. The horns are all honking at ME. At some point I see a sign for the Holland Tunnel, and, sniveling badly now, shaking, I veer right (or left, I no longer remember), shoot into its yawning maw and down under the sullen waters of the Hudson River (where, for amusement, I used to fish with a stick for condoms to throw at Morris as he sat reading Flaubert along the bank). I am evacuated out the tunnel's posterior orifice into New Jersey, where I scurry along with all the other flotsam and jetsam toward a major western drainage—the Pennsylvania Turnpike.

Which brings me to the point. In the dream I wake up. In reality I did not stop driving until I was somewhere in Oklahoma. Forty hours later and another dawn under my crimson lids, I finally stopped the car and stepped outside, did a slow 360 and looked off in every direction at . . . nothing. Blessed nothing. The horizon. I felt as if someone had lifted a pack off my back and pulled cotton out of my nose. Space. Boundless, limitless, endless, infinite, shoreless, trackless, pathless space. I felt I was home. Or at least very close.

In a way the collection of essays contained herein grow out of this little epiphany, and out of the attempt, pursued both consciously and unconsciously over a longer period of time than I like to admit, to understand what it is that spiritually sustains me, and where on this planet that most seems to occur. The observation that if you don't know *where* you are, you don't know *who* you are is, I think, Wendell Berry's, but it's an idea implicit in the work of many great Americans who have written thoughtfully about our native landscape. It is central to any understanding I have of Henry David Thoreau, John Muir, Aldo Leopold, Sigurd Olson, Joseph Wood Krutch, Olaus Murie, Sally Carrighar, Colin Fletcher, Wendell Berry, Ann Zwinger, Edward Abbey, Annie Dillard, Peter Matthiessen, Barry Lopez (to name only a few authors I admire), and it is the keystone in virtually all of the novels, essays, historical studies, and historical biographies written by my father, Wallace Stegner—a body of work that over the years has had an increasing influence on my own interests and pursuits. For my father the American West was never just the subject. It was an accumulation of associations, memories, histories; an inheritance of values, attitudes, and beliefs; spiritual and physical sustenance. It is to him that I owe whatever small understanding I myself possess in matters of place and regional self, and so it is to him that this book is gratefully and lovingly dedicated.

Some of these pieces have been published in *The Atlantic Monthly, California Magazine, Wilderness,* and *The North Dakota Review.* They are an eclectic gathering, to be sure, unevenly representational in a geographic sense, though I believe they contain a broader perspective of the American West today (albeit seen through one set of glass eyes, darkly) than the limitations of their physical range might imply. At least I hope so. They are often unapologetic in their disapproval of everything that doesn't subscribe to my particular ontological notions, but what can I do? As a friend of mine once said, "I don't want to be reasonable, I just want to be right." To which, in a spirit of humility nowhere else found in this book, I offer the amendment—I just want to be right with a small *r* and a gram of humor.

Outposts of Eden

PART ONE

Basin, Range, and Plateau

1

Desert Solitaire

*F*OR THE THIRD WEEK in a row the mid-morning temperature in Parker is over 110 degrees. While I wait for gas I stand in the shade of a Mobil station canopy, squinting across the sagebrush to the line of tamarisk and willow along the Colorado River that marks the border between Arizona and southern California. Beyond the river lies the great desert, twenty-five million acres of barren, bleak terrain that makes up one-quarter of the land surface of America's most populated and geophysically diverse state. Three deserts, actually: the Colorado, Mojave, and Great Basin, each blending into the other and distinguished by major increases in elevation as one moves north. The Colorado desert (generally below three thousand feet) extends from the Mexican border to an imaginary line drawn between Los Angeles and Phoenix. The Mojave continues for some two hundred miles north before giving way, in turn, to the higher, colder Basin and Range province associated primarily with Nevada and western Utah. Colder, it should be said, is a relative term.

A growing sensation at the top of my cherubic cheeks begins to announce itself as the searing metal frames of my glasses undergoing rapid thermogenesis outside the air-conditioned cab of my truck. I remove them when the temple wires become molten and my sideburns begin to fry. A damp, pink man with a bumper sticker on his pickup that reads "Sierra Club, Kiss My Axe" fills his tank in the aisle next to me and comes back to polish the windshield of the boat he's towing—a candy-apple red projectile with a white tuck-and-roll interior and a half dozen chrome pipes sticking out of the engine casing like rocket launchers. He observes my California plates and asks if I, too, am in Parker for the jet boat races. I tell him no, I'm just down checking out my desert—seeing if it needs watering or anything like that.

"Your desert," he says. "Ha ha ha."

I don't know what's so funny. It is my desert. It's *his* desert, too. Over three-quarters of the region is federally owned lands, some of it (two and a half million acres) in national monuments and state parks, a bit more (three million acres) in military reservations, the rest of it (twelve and a half million acres) Bureau of Land Management (BLM) territory administered for the American people by the Department of the Interior. Except where the Pentagon plays furtively with explosives and supersonic toys it is "public domain," though the general public's interest in *this* domain seldom extends beyond calculations of speed and distance—how fast it can be crossed.

Not surprising. The California desert is replete with

uninviting place names like Death Valley, Devil's Playground, Furnace Creek (where the hottest temperature officially recorded in the United States occurred on July 10, 1913—134 degrees Fahrenheit, in the shade), Badwater (where it is historically four degrees hotter than Furnace Creek, and where there is no shade), Funeral Mountains, Dead Mountains, Styx, Poison Wells. While it is actually more inhabited than one might expect— particularly where San Bernardino and San Diego have sprawled eastward into the Coachella and Imperial valleys around Palm Springs, Indio, and El Centro—settlement is sparse by any standards. And the majority are contained in a relatively small area southeast of Los Angeles. The interior is not for everybody. Practically anybody.

Certainly it is not for my friend at the Mobil station in Parker. He tells me he crossed "all that greasewood" in four hours flat and advises me to do the same, then tows his boat off toward the local marina to spend a restful weekend tearing up and down the Colorado, spewing gasoline fumes and oil slicks, splitting the quietude of canyon and river with the screaming fury of high tech engines wound to their breaking point. Some fun. Unfortunately he is an increasingly common type. He has his counterparts in the operators of off-road vehicles (motorcycles, dune buggies, four-wheel drive jeeps, trail bikes) who are as destructive to the desert ecology as he is to the river. Together they represent a phylum of American whose love of the outdoors is expressed solely by the various ways they tear it up with an internal combustion engine. They constitute as great a threat to wilderness as all the mining, energy, and livestock interests who destroy it for profit.

Ah well, another grumping environmentalist. I cross the bridge into California and head west toward Joshua Tree National Monument, one of three major desert parks in the region and about midway between the Arizona border and the Pacific coast. A hot wind buffets the truck, whipping the creosote brush along the road, whirling off across the sand like some mad dust devil executing entrechats and pliés through the cactus. Nasty stuff, creosote brush, and not to be confused with that sweet-smelling inhabitant of high altitude deserts—sage. The creosote bush, also known as greasewood, exudes a toxin into the ground to kill off all potential competitors for the infrequent rains that sustain life. It will poison its own offspring, given half a chance, and tastes so foul even cattle don't like to eat it. Which no doubt explains why it is the most conspicuous plant throughout these arid lands.

All around me the dun colored plain is periodically broken by low ranges of mountains that seem as barren and inhospitable as the parched ground from which they rise—or from which I presume they rise. A hundred feet in front of my bumper the highway vanishes in a mercuric line of shimmering heat and I am surrounded by an opalescent sea of thermal waves that ebb and flow with each change in the road. At times it seems more like crossing an estuary than a desert. Cholla, yucca, beaver-tail cactus, and the ubiquitous greasewood poke up above the puddles. Somewhere to my right the Colorado River aqueduct snakes through jagged ridges that appear to float on the basin floor like islands. Big Maria Mountains, Turtle Mountains, Old Woman Mountains, Coxcomb Mountains.

Mountains? Yes, indeed. Some of them four and five

thousand feet high. The present configuration of the Mojave is thought to have been formed during the Cenozoic era from uplifting associated with movement of the many thrust faults that strike across it in a predominantly north-south direction. The Garlock and San Andreas faults are the most infamous, but there are at least thirty others of less impressive dimension. Sometime during the Oligocene epoch the earth's crust, tortured by the stress of plate movement, broke into great blocks that were forced upward to form the high ranges and deep troughs that were then subjected to forty million years of erosional processes. The troughs between the ranges gradually filled with material that crumbled down from the slopes, and a once mountainous topography was all but erased, buried in its own debris. And the process is hardly complete, as any desert traveler can plainly see. Wherever these old molars have been wrinkled and cut by the forces of wind and rain, alluvial fans flow out of the canyon mouths like gravel aprons, sloping gently toward the center of the basins they have been slowly filling since the last days of the dinosaur.

II

It is late when I arrive at Joshua Tree and I am forced to lay out my gear by the lights of my truck. The Park Service provides a table and a fire pit with a grate, but I converted my operation to a propane camp stove long ago, and have no need of these amenities. Not very aesthetic, propane, but it saves scrambling over five hundred acres of rattlesnakes and scorpions in search of the twelve remaining twigs in the area not discovered by previous campers. It also saves me from contributing to one of the less appealing features of the modern American campsite—a pigsty of charcoal and ashes ringed by a splatter of half-burned garbage. People who otherwise understand that it is wicked to leave a sack of trash in their wake will nevertheless try to burn wet newspaper, soggy lettuce, steak bones, beer cans, gin bottles, and other assorted nonflammable components of their wilderness experience. Wood fires should be banned from the national parks, never mind how cheerfully they dispel creatures who go bump in the night.

Joshua Tree encompasses an area of nearly a half million acres and provides within its boundaries an excellent contrast between Mojave and Colorado desert ecosystems. The eastern half of the monument lies below three thousand feet and is dominated by creosote brush, small stands of spidery ocotillo (that looks like some kind of multilimbed sea worm) and jumping cholla, a deceptively benign-looking cactus with a single trunk and a number of short lateral branches on top that are so closely set with straw colored spines they appear soft and cuddly. They aren't. In the higher, slightly cooler areas, twisted rock and granite monoliths create a broken terrain where the *yucca brevifolia* thrives. Early Mormon travelers crossing the California desert thought it looked like Joshua leading the Israelites out of the wilderness and so named it in his honor. It looks like a bad drug trip to me. Especially those samples bordering my campsite, their twisted, contorted branches silhouetted against the night sky. The Joshua tree is a member of the lily family (which it in no respect resembles), grows to thirty feet, and when looked at in the daylight reminds me strangely of thorn trees dotting the Serengeti

Plain of northwestern Tanzania—widely spaced, solitary, yet totally dominating the low horizon.

Because I am not clouding the atmosphere with wood smoke I am treated after dinner to a bowl full of stars to light my way into bed. Leave my tennis shoes in the back of the truck to discourage wandering scorpions. Pull a tarp over my sleeping bag and lie on top because it is still too hot for covers. A coyote barks somewhere up on Sheep Pass, answered by a relative off in the low hills to my left. Good hunting, guys. Keep the racket down. A meteor drops like a hot spark, punctuating consciousness. Later, around the first light of dawn, I wake for a moment and catch in the corner of my eye a shadow trotting through the piñon scrub separating my camp from the park road. Friend coyote heading home with what appears to be the remains of an unlucky jackrabbit.

Unless one has the night vision of an owl, and a disposition for wandering around dark places where every scrap of plant life is a pincushion of spines, needles, thorns, one is not likely to see much in the way of desert fauna. But it's out there, and in a profusion that would startle most travelers who regard the Mojave as a wasteland. Coyotes, of course, and bobcat, desert bighorn sheep, desert tortoise, antelope ground squirrel (often mistaken for a chipmunk), round-tailed squirrel, grasshopper mouse, white-footed mouse, harvest mouse, little spiny pocket mouse (who comes about the size of a walnut and can jump three feet in the air), cactus mouse, brown-footed wood rat, dusky-footed brush rat, and everybody's favorite—the kangaroo rat. This fuzzy little rodent with feet the size of a spatula looks as if he was invented by a Walt Disney cartoonist. When I am finally forced from my bed by the bright morning sun I find his tracks in the sand all around my sleeping bag. Checking me out to see if I'm edible, the nocturnal snoop. It's comforting to recall that he is strictly vegetarian. Not so comforting however, the discovery that my tennis shoes have been kidnapped from the tailgate of the truck. Probably lie murdered under some prickly pear. Unlucky jackrabbit, indeed.

III

Leaving the park after breakfast I head north over the Sheephole Mountains and across Bristol Dry Lake to Amboy, a tiny railroad junction for the Atchison, Topeka, and Santa Fe line, and a place of residence for a number of workers who mine the lake bottom for calcium chloride. This is truly a less accommodating landscape than the surface of the moon. Bristol is like almost all the lakes scattered throughout the Mojave and Great Basin, internal drainage bottoms, dry on the surface and bottomless muck underneath. Trenches are dug as deep as twenty feet into the sludge, allowed to fill with subsurface water from which salts are then precipitated. Pools of alkaline scum. Chemical slag heaps that look like dirty snow. At the northern end of the basin the dark cinder cone of the Amboy crater projects its perfect volcanic snout above the flats—a relative newcomer, geologists believe, having exploded and spewed its molten lava over a five-mile area within the last thousand years.

Small wonder, I suppose, that a lot of people regard proposals for the protection of this kind of country as a dementia of the environmental lunatic fringe. The California Desert Conservation Area Plan, mandated by

Congress in 1976, written by the Bureau of Land Management after five years of "intensive" study, approved in 1981, has been under constant attack from mining interests, livestock interests, and off-road vehicle (ORV) clubs who would like to (and probably will) amend it out of existence. Particularly operators of motorized gadgets who seem to feel that it is their God-given right to run their machinery whenever and wherever they please, regardless of their effect on wildlife habitat and fragile soils and plants. "I don't tell you where to drive your car, do I?" one truculent dune buggy owner tells me during an inadvertent lunch counter interview I conduct over an Amboy burger in the town of the same name.

"Give me your address," I tell him. "Next time I'm in your town I'll come over and drive it on your lawn."

The Amboy burger is a discouraging affair. Preparation seems to have coincided with the birth of the crater for which it is named. One more salvo at the dune buggy driver and I belch on over Granite Pass toward Kelso, Cima, and the Ivanpah Mountains along the Nevada border. Somewhere between the Devil's Playground and the lava beds north of Kelso I stop to stretch the legs and climb a low gravel hump for a better view of the great sand dunes that lie in a basin between the Bristol and Soda Mountains. I am, frankly, in the process of contributing to the moisture content of this arid land when the ground under me seems to list to starboard and then suddenly subside about a foot and a half. I find myself on my knees looking at a network of small holes my blundering presence has evidently destroyed. Kangaroo rats again. They have honeycombed the area with the burrows, and I can hear the local inhabitants chiding me for my intrusion from deep in their tunnels, a sound that reminds me of the flutter of quail wings.

Two-thirds of the mammals that inhabit the California desert are rodents or gnawing animals, survivors because they have adapted to heat and drought in ways that other creatures could not. They come out of their holes only after dark. Unlike their bungling visitor they pass very little urine. They have no sweat glands and consequently lose no body liquid through perspiration. Many never drink at all, metabolizing what water they need out of the seeds and grasses on which they live. In a region that receives less than ten inches of rainfall a year (much of it less than five, and some of it as little as an inch and a half) this is a biological endowment that is critical. Sorry about the damage here, folks. I hope you have insurance.

IV

The dirt road skirts Kessler Peak and joins Interstate 15 just west of Nipton. Coming over the pass between the Clark and Mescal ranges at about five o'clock, I find myself faced with the prospect of continuing an eighty-mile-an-hour freeway frenzy straight into the setting sun (along with thousands of fun-loving Las Vegas weekenders heading home to Los Angeles), or of pulling off onto another of the dirt mining roads that meander back down through Piute Valley to Cima and waiting until the traffic lets up. It has been a long day's drive. A quiet hour in the shade of a juniper tree seems justifiable, and I have no deadlines, no need to debate my choices. Besides, the panorama across the mountains of the East Mojave is spectacular just now. Majestic blue ranges piling one on top of another, a golden light behind the last spinal ridge, a crazy, teatime moon rising over Crescent Peak across the Nevada border to challenge the sunset.

It was encouraging to read in this morning's paper that Senator Alan Cranston has introduced a bill before Congress that would (among other things) turn this whole slide show into a national park, legislate the view, so to speak, and protect both landscape and ecosystem against further economic development and mindless, motorized "recreation." To say the Cranston bill represents a giant step toward establishing in law the aesthetic and spiritual values long claimed by environmentalists for the Mojave is to absurdly understate its importance. To pass by and not stop to peer out across its smoky expanse, even for an hour, is to commit an impious act.

Kodachrome moments notwithstanding, the California desert has often been reduced, as my Mobil chum in Parker suggested, to little more than a barren, bleak, broiling gravel pit through which the wise traveler rapidly accelerates on the way to more temperate climes. Not everybody's cup of tea. An arid wasteland. A moonscape. A cracked, parched, malignant home of sidewinders and scraggly plants. Although it comprises nearly one-quarter of the state, fewer people live in its entire 39,000 square miles (an area roughly the size of East Germany) than in Sacramento, the state capital. Of course, about three-quarters of its total area is "locked up," as the anti-preservationist saying goes, in those military reservations, national monuments, state parks, and BLM lands, but there are still seven million acres left for expansion. Or so it might seem.

The truth is that the California desert has seen a great deal more expansion, development, and unrestricted use than its fragile environment can stand. The truth is that arid land receiving less than ten to twelve inches of rainfall a year is *not* a hospitable environment for human beings—unless they alter it in major ways. Meaning water it, air-condition it, pave it, shade it with exotic, imported trees—all of which generally comes at the environmental expense of some other region. But it *is* the home of the kit fox and the kangaroo rat, the cottontail, chuckawalla, and centipede, the cactus wren, turkey vulture, grantcatcher, roadrunner, and shrike, the desert tortoise and the desert hare—the home of nearly a thousand species of plants and animals, all of whom depend on the integrity of its ecosystem and none of whom can withstand uncontrolled intrusions by man. Particularly man with a machine. The truth is that the desert is not "locked up" enough.

I could get an argument I suppose. The view this evening from under the tailgate of the truck (my portable Juniper tree) does not suggest much about human activity out there in the general direction of the Providence and New York mountains. Evening has washed definition from the eroded slopes of the ranges; great alluvial fans flowing from their canyons pour as smooth as pond water into the dark basins below. The most distant escarpments of the Piute Range to the southeast and the Kelso and Bristol mountains to the southwest float like haze above a receding line of ridges. Seems pretty empty. But man is most definitely out there, digging his minerals, cutting roads, overgrazing livestock, hounding rocks, and roaring around in four-wheel drive vehicles.

Most particularly roaring around in four-wheel drive vehicles. Not far from here in Dove Springs Canyon, I recall, it took ORV users a short ten years to completely denude 543 acres of land, and tear up the plant cover on an additional thousand acres. Bureau of Land Management studies done at the time estimated that by 1988 at least 1,600 acres would be completely stripped of vegetation.

Which is not surprising when one considers the general level of social development displayed by a good many "off-road" practitioners. Like the three I watch bounding up the long slope below me, grinding through gullies, smashing greasewood, trailing a mile-long plume of dust in their wake. They reach the top, veer onto the mining road, and roar past my evening meditation like something out of a Mad Max nightmare, burying me under an acre of sand, rock, and shards of rabbit brush torn from the desert pavement by their screaming transports. Three belligerent-looking troglodytes in plastic goggles with plastic pots on their heads. Spent a hard day out in the dunes churning up the burrows of kangaroo rats and kit foxes, no doubt. Observe the splayed feet for mashing brake and clutch pedals, the hairy forearms for strangling handlebars, the porcine, shock-absorbing buttocks, the opposable thumbs. Observe the havoc they wreak on the delicate soil, soil that in this climate takes a millennium to form. Good day to you, too, gentlemen. I hope that when you reach the interstate you may experience what a famous outlaw biker once described as the ultimate in a two-cycle thrill—a high-torque, full-throttle, speedwobble across the highway divider into the oncoming grill of an eighteen-wheeler.

I hope, actually, for the Cranston bill—a less violent resolution to the problem of desert abuse. I hope it is passed into law before the whole twenty-five million acres is churned into slurry and washed into the Salton Sea, though it will undoubtedly take two or three years and a major struggle on the part of environmental organizations to see it through. If it is passed—*when* it is passed—The California Desert Protection Act will establish Mojave National Park in much of the territory stretching out here before me—territory currently designated the East Mojave National Scenic Area. The park, 1.6 million acres bordered on the north by Interstate 15 and on the south by Interstate 40, and extending roughly from an imaginary line between Baker and Amboy east to the Arizona border, will include the Devil's Playground and the Kelso Dunes, the Providence and New York mountains, at least four dry lakes, a number of volcanic cones, the largest Joshua tree forest in the world, several major petroglyph sites, seven hundred species of plants (most of them prickly), and three hundred species of animals (most of them four-legged). Park status will protect all this from abuse by two-legged animals. It will, moreover, relieve custodial responsibility from its current mismanager, the BLM.

The act will transfer to California some 20,500 acres of federal lands inside the boundaries of Red Rock Canyon State Park in the El Paso Mountains above Fremont Valley, resolving in the process an unfulfilled "agreement" made between the state and the BLM in 1969. It will also redesignate Death Valley and Joshua Tree national monuments, upgrading them to national parks, and expanding their boundaries to include the Eureka and Saline valleys northwest of Death Valley and the Eagle Mountains southeast of Joshua Tree. Apart from including ecosystems that are important to the existing sanctuaries (ecosystems that should have been included when the boundaries were originally established in the 1930s), park status for these two areas will really only improve their "public image" and have no effect on their management or management policies.

Perhaps the most important feature of the Senator's bill is its intention to designate 4.5 million acres of the public domain as wilderness, upgrading a somewhat more *modest* (cough) BLM proposal, and finally implementing what Congress had in mind twenty-two years ago when it passed The Wilderness Act of 1964. That legislation, along with its step-child, the Federal Land Policy Management Act (FLPMA), directed all government agencies charged with custodial obligations on public lands to stop thinking of natural resource management as a synonym for economic exploitation and to start thinking about the concept of multiple use. Designated wilderness areas, Congress said, "shall be administered . . . in such a manner as will leave them unimpaired for future use and enjoyment as *wilderness* and so as to provide for the protection of these areas, [and] the preservation of their *wilderness character*" [italics mine]. Meaning no commercial development, no roads, no structures, and no internal combustion engines. Meaning—for a lot of people—no use. Because a lot of people have yet to become acquainted with shank's mare.

Those who have yet to become acquainted with the BLM might suppose that, as a branch of the Department of the Interior, as the management company in charge of watching over 274 million acres of the public's land, the agency might have those twelve and a half million acres under its jurisdiction in California *already* in protective custody. Additional legislation establishing more wilderness areas, national parks, sanctuaries, historic sites, what have you, would be simply redundant—no? No. Emphatically, no. Directed by FLPMA to inventory its holdings and make recommendations on areas meeting the criteria for "wilderness" (areas that provide "opportunities for solitude or for primitive and unconfined recreation," and contain "geological, ecological, scientific, scenic or historical" values), the BLM was only able to come up with a meager 2.1 million acres—a figure it has since managed to reduce some twelve percent to 1.84 million acres. The agency's 1982 amendments to the original Desert Plan, incredibly, eliminated recommendations for the Panamint Dunes, Greenwater Valley, Bighorn Mountains, Sheephole Mountains, Saline Valley, Kelso Dunes, the Resting Spring and Nopah ranges.

Why? Who knows why. Certainly not because the above real estate fails to provide opportunities for solitude and primitive recreation. Not because the parcels lack geological, ecological, or scenic value. Cynics might suggest they were found unsuitable because mining companies expressed a competitive interest, ranchers howled for increased grazing allotments on deteriorating range, ORV clubs demanded more access—unrestricted access, unlimited access—as they trashed the areas they already had. Cynics might even suggest that the Department of the Interior, as constituted by the Reagan Administration, has *always* pursued a policy of open resistance to protective legislation. Whatever the reasons, the Cranston bill, when passed, should make federal foot-dragging, evasion, and noncompliance with the law a lot harder. It will certainly "lock things up" more effectively than they are at present. And it will no doubt completely unhinge the already hysterical opposition to wilderness. It's something we may just have to learn to live with.

V

The teatime moon has won its argument with the setting sun. Time to move on. The teal-wing mountains have gone black, their bright backdrop turned copper, lavender, indigo, before losing the cosmetic blush and melting into the etched lines of the ridge tops. Back on the highway, I am reduced to white knuckles and bulging eyeballs, hurtling along the center lane, terrified I am about to become a scrap of Toyota ham in a big rig sandwich. I can hear them downshift behind me as we fly over the summit at Mexican Well and rocket down into the Shadow Valley toward Baker, Barstow, San Bernardino.

Humanoids are as abundant as kangaroo rats in Baker, a mid-Mojave pit stop along Interstate 15 that cuts northeast from Los Angeles and ends at the Canadian border near Glacier National Park. Cadillacs, Lincolns, Buicks, motor homes, trailers, stream through town, most headed for the gambling pens in Las Vegas—HOWDY PARDNER—windows closed, air conditioners blowing frost into the perms of brittle-eyed gents in seizure suits, while Ms. Spandex sucks down another Virginia Slim and rides, bored, in the passenger seat, waiting for the desert to pass, waiting for glitter gulch to appear on the horizon. No biological adaptation here. And all of this watched by the highway patrolman in shiny black boots and Vuarnet shades who waits hopefully on the interstate apron at the edge of town, engine running, ticket book at the ready. HOWDY PARDNER.

I stop only long enough for gas, then hightail it north through bone-dry hills toward Death Valley. The Great Basin Indians who first came here around a thousand years ago called it *Tomesha,* a word that supposedly means "ground afire." By rights it isn't a valley at all, but a graben—a depression that occurs between two parallel faults when the earth's convulsions force great blocks of tortured, twisted rock into mountains. Death Valley is bounded by the Amargosa and Panamint ranges, the peaks of which rise on the east to five and six thousand feet, and on the west as high as 11,000 feet. Between the two lies the collapsed sinkhole of salt, mud, gravel, sand, and blast furnace temperatures that most people think is the major attraction of the California desert, and some would argue is the major attraction of any desert in the world. But then most people see it largely from behind the tinted glass of a climate-controlled vehicle—a visual rather than a thermal experience.

Spectacle is perhaps a more accurate word than *attraction.* Whether Death Valley inspires one's poetic imagination or makes one shudder and step on the gas is pretty much a matter of disposition. I'm of both persuasions. Coming into it from the south, after a night unwittingly spent camped on an anthill, the mountains seem to fall in on each other, tumbling down from 3,315 feet at Salsbury Pass to a point on the valley floor that is below sea level—254 feet below sea level, to be exact, the lowest point in the United States. Parallel escarpments over a mile high are separated by a dry chemical lake nearly a hundred miles long and ten miles wide, all of it shaking and wobbling in the saffron heat of mid-afternoon. The overwhelming impression is that nothing is alive here in this chaos of warped and folded rock except a few stalks of creosote brush, pickleweed, and salt grass.

This is not true, exactly. The famous botanist Frederick Vernon Colville, whose 1891 expedition into Death Valley is still the foundation of all ecological study in the eastern California desert, listed 1,200 species and varieties of plants in the area, and when one remembers that the park traverses vegetation zones from the lower Sonoran to the subalpine, these numbers are not difficult to believe. But then I'm told that the rocks lying at the base of the Black Mountains right over there to my right are early Precambrian—which is to say anywhere from a billion to 600 million years old—and I believe that too. With about the same degree of understanding and capacity to conceptualize. I'll believe anything, but I still say it looks mighty dead down here.

From a point at the foot of the pass where the valley floor narrows between the Black Mountains and Owlshead Mountain I look north across a vast, smoky, pale distance hemmed in by steeply sloping alluvial fans, sulfur-colored walls shading into mauve, rose, charcoal, and creased by a thousand welts and folds. Beautiful and ugly. Inviting and terrifying. They look sore in this light, like a nasty bruise. They look cracked and parched like the rotting hides of indecipherable, hairless animals. They look like some kind of malignancy that could draw me in and snuff me out.

Evidently the Park Service thinks so too. It has erected a wooden box by the side of the road with a sign attached, *Death Valley Survival Hints.* Hints? Why so coy? Why not just come right out with it? For survival stay in the shade and drink lots of water. Better yet, stop in at your friendly Fred Harvey bourgeois burrow at Furnace Creek Inn and Stovepipe Wells. Belly up to the bar for a cool one. Take a cue from the snakes and lizards and stay in a hole until dark.

Furnace Creek, one of the two places in the national monument that offer accommodations (Fred Harvey, concessionaire), is an oasis of date palm, cottonwood, and tamarisk. The springs that irrigate this small area in the center of the valley bubble up from an underground aquifer that lies along the base of the nearby Funeral Mountains. They are the only significant potable water resource available, but they are sufficient (or so I am told by a park ranger) to provide for the ten thousand visitors who arrive at peak usage times over the Christmas and Easter holidays, as well as for normal consumption on a year-round basis. How long this can continue is anyone's guess. How big is that subterranean lake? With average rainfall in Death Valley at 1.7 inches a year, how fast can an aquifer recharge? How many showers and flushes and trips to the ice machine are there left before Furnace Creek Springs burps up one last quart of sulfuric brine and goes dry?

Well, for the moment, anyway, we have palm groves and lawns, an olympic-size swimming pool, an eighteen-hole golf course, stables, bikes, lighted tennis courts—all of which, the Fred Harvey brochure proudly tells us, "is just the beginning of Furnace Creek Resort life." One is tempted to ask what a "resort" has to do with a national park or monument, and to wonder whether we really need golf, tennis, and poolside dining in the world's hottest, driest place. Why is an inability to distinguish between a natural preserve and a playground endemic to the American mind? Some American minds. Departments of the Interior minds. No wonder a night at the inn costs $150 for a single.

I take my curmudgeonly carcass out near the foot of the Cottonwood Mountains, squat over my propane stove and cook a surly can of beans. Tomorrow I'll head west, over the Panamints and down into the trough of the Panamint Valley, over the southern extension of the White Mountains and down into the Owens Valley where the great wall of the Sierra Nevada rises abruptly out of the shadscale and sagebrush to block in its rain-shadow everything that lies to the east for nearly five hundred miles. The ultimate range, and personally responsible for this gravel pit where I cook my supper. Tonight, however, I'm willing to forgive. I take my after-dinner cigar and stroll a bit out into Mesquite Flat toward the dunes above Stovepipe Wells. Scraggly plant life gives way to sand, gracefully embroidered here and there with the tiny tracks of circus beetles, and as evening settles down the last of the sunlight sets fire to a few high wisps of cloud, turning the mangled old ridge of the Amargosa Range into one radiant moment etched against the darkening backdrop of space. Not a bad piece of real estate. Glad I own it.

2

Bitter and Fatal Waters

B ELOW THE TOWN OF BRIDGEPORT, Highway 395 cuts through a gentle valley between the western slope of the Toiyabe National Forest and the slopes of Bodie Mountain, climbs onward from Little Mormon Meadow to Conway Summit (elevation 8,138), and drops abruptly 1,800 feet into the expansive Mono Basin. The wind blowing down from Virginia Lakes carries the scent of pines freshened by granite and ice, sharp contrast to the alkali dust devils swirling across the Mono Valley toward the basin and range country of Nevada. From the vista just below the summit one looks across the startling lunar waters of Mono Lake to rows of volcanic cones lying like mollusks amidst a gray expanse of sage and pumice. Thirty miles to the south Glass Mountain pokes up above the broken plain of graveled desert, and farther still the hazy imprint of the White Mountains, eastern boundary of Owens Valley and home of one of the oldest living things on the face of the earth, a

4,600-year-old bristlecone pine, beginning life as ancient Babylon fell. Flanking Mono County to the west, the unimaginable barricade of the Sierra Nevada.

I camp out in the sagebrush beneath the Mono craters one early spring afternoon, muttering to myself about the seasons of solitude and the cost in thermal units of wandering around with nothing cozier than a tube tent and a down bag leaking feathers. Pumice Valley they call this hardscrabble ground just south of Lee Vining ("Gateway to Yosemite"), and there's no mystery in the name. From here Mono Lake is the focal point, sixty square miles of Ice Age waters so dense with chlorides, carbonates, and sulfates that it is three times saltier than seawater and eighty times as alkaline. Strange rock formations known as tufa dot its shores. Knobby spires, "giant towers of cemented cauliflower"—however they have been variously described, they seem an obvious invention of Jules Verne's imagination. Like the stalactites and stalagmites it closely resembles, tufa is composed primarily of calcite, a mineral produced when calcium in freshwater springs welling up from the bottom of the lake combines with the carbonates in its brine.

"The bitter and fatal waters of the lake," said the Sacramento *Daily Union* in 1868, "render it literally a dead sea and all of its surroundings—wild, gloomy, foreboding—are suggestive of sterility and death." The *Daily Union* reporter must have visited Mono sometime between November and March, actually *anytime* when winter, its onslaught or aftermath, has driven away obvious signs of life, or he would never have offered such a vacant opinion. Dead it is not. Although it may support only a few species of invertebrate life, it does so in such abundance that it qualifies as one of the most *life-productive* lakes in the world. "At peak densities," writes biologist David Gaines of the Mono Lake Committee, "over 50,000 brine shrimp crowd a cubic yard of lakewater; the overall population exceeds four trillion individuals and weighs over six million pounds dry weight. Brine flies darken the shore for mile after mile; four thousand have been tallied in a single square foot."

Had I wings and a beak instead of feet and teeth I would not find myself squatting over a pan of Spam and some wizened potatoes. I'd be dining on algae, brine shrimp and brine flies. Not a varied diet, perhaps, but an improvement on Spam. Sufficient, at least, to attract just about every species of shorebird, grebe and duck in North America. For the California gull Mono Lake is a critical habitat. Ninety-five percent of the breeding population of the state's endangered snowy plover lay their eggs along its alkaline shores. And 150,000 Wilson's phalaropes, 50,000 northern phalaropes, and nearly a million eared grebes stop while migrating from Canada and the Northwest to feed before continuing south for the winter. Some are believed to fly nonstop as far away as Argentina. Without Mono Lake their journey might never be completed.

Dead it is not; though like the Kuzedika Paiute culture that thrived in this region until the 1870s, it may be pushed to the edge of extinction. For hundreds of years the Kuzedika harvested the brine fly pupae and larvae along the shores of the lake to dry for meal, gathered piñon nuts from the nearby forests, and dug for roots and bulbs in the meadows beneath the sheer mountain walls. But by the end of the 1860s miners from the western slopes of the Sierra had spread eastward into the Mono Basin in such numbers (15,000 in the now-ghost town of Bodie alone) that the Kuzedika were reduced to a few scattered families, their game destroyed, their forests cut for cordwood and mine timbers, their meadows ruined by overgrazing. Today there is concern that even the brine shrimp and brine flies may not survive the continued development of the West—not mining this time, for the booms have all gone bust—but water diversion to more populated areas of the state.

When I last stayed here over five years ago the streambed just down the hill from my camp, once a major feeder creek for Mono Lake, was dry, and not because of the time of year or the vagaries of the snowpack up in the Sierra. The expanse of cracking flats spreading out from its mouth and around the lake were testimony to its co-option by the folks down south to assist them in their effort to make the desert bloom. Their desert, not this one. In 1940, when the Los Angeles Department of Water and Power (DWP) completed an extension of its Owens Valley Aqueduct into the Mono Basin and diverted all but one of its tributary streams to the deserts of southern California, the lake began receding, its total area decreasing over the years from 85 to 60 square miles, its depth reduced by 45 feet, its shore an expanding belt of alkaline mud that dried in the summer months and swirled skyward in vast, choking dust storms. Airline pilots occasionally mistook those chemical clouds for volcanic eruptions, others for towering geysers of steam rivaling Old Faithful in Yellowstone. As the waters receded, a land bridge between the mainland and Negit Island emerged, opening the nesting ground for thirty to forty thousand gulls to predators. In 1979 approximately 33,000 California gulls nested on Negit; in 1985 a Point Reyes Bird Observatory researcher, David

Shuford, counted 92. Many of the Negit colony relocated to smaller rocks and islets, to be sure, but these habitats provided almost no vegetation or cover from summer sun, exposure to which gull chicks seem to have difficulty surviving. In 1981 ninety percent of the hatchlings died, though whether this was due to exposure or to the concurrent collapse of the brine shrimp population, or both, is not altogether clear.

The salinity of Mono Lake's already briny water has about doubled since diversions began. The most recent (and comprehensive) water balance model done by a Hayward State University graduate student named Peter Vorster suggests that brine shrimp and brine fly larvae might withstand salt levels approximately twice Mono Lake's current level of nine percent, but at salinity levels of only thirteen percent these invertebrates will suffer a dramatic decline in growth rate and reproductive success. According to Vorster's model, if the DWP continues to divert water at its current rate, we are only ten or fifteen years from that point. Salinities in excess of twenty percent will almost certainly wipe out the entire population—and when the invertebrates go, the vertebrates will not be far behind. And no one is sure how tolerant the lake's *algae* may be to high levels of salinity. Should the algae die, the entire food chain would collapse.

But the streambed below my camp is not dry this year. Rush Creek has water in it for the fifth season in a row—not a lot, one must admit, but enough to fill its bed a foot or two feet deep and make a racket as it sings over gravel bars and around the tangled deadfall. I follow it upstream in the direction of the high moraines whence it comes, flailing through dense willows, busting my ankles on granite boulders, and wishing at each pool and cutbank that I had my fly rod. With my fly rod I could spend the afternoon catching cottonwoods and unsnarling monofilament spaghetti. Then I could contribute to Fish and Game with a big fat fine for angling out of season. Another big fat fine. Still, they are tempting, those rainbows and browns I see darting into the shadows and under the rocks.

This waterway was a dry wash in 1981. Then a couple years of excessively high snowpack required the DWP to dump water from its upstream dam to prevent overflow, Rush Creek was briefly alive again, and an amazing thing happened. The trout returned. According to Dick Dahlgren of California Trout, by 1984 there were 30,000 fish in Rush Creek, some 7,500 per mile in the upper stretches. Now this seems to me like a lot of pisciculture in pretty short order. Surely nobody would have sneaked in here and *planted* them. Would they?

In 1984 Dahlgren and Cal Trout, along with the Mammouth Fly Rodders, the Mono Lake Committee, and the National Audubon Society filed a lawsuit against the DWP to force continued releasing of water into Rush Creek. The lawsuit was based on Fish and Game codes that require dam owners to provide sufficient flows to maintain downstream fisheries in "good condition," the California Environmental Quality Act that requires an environmental impact report (EIR) for new projects, and the 1983 California Supreme Court ruling that Mono Lake, under the doctrine of public trust, must be protected "as far as feasible"—a decision that paved the way for current and future challenges to Los Angeles' right to take as much water from other people's buckets as it wants. Recognizing the substantial concerns of the city, seventeen percent of whose water comes from the

Mono Basin, the court nevertheless ruled that human and environmental considerations under the doctrine of public trust are an integral part of California's system of water law and must be taken into account in the allocation of water resources. The license granted Los Angeles is not inviolable, the court seemed to say; the survival of brine shrimp and gull chicks must be also considered before they are lost to growth and development.

The DWP, naturally, takes issue with this opinion, arguing over the interpretation of "feasible," insisting that an annual decision to divert water does not constitute a "new" project and requires no EIR, claiming that a 1940 agreement with Fish and Game exempts it from the law, denying the obvious relationship of Rush Creek and the lake it feeds. Meanwhile, as things are being hashed out by judges and lawyers (a process that will undoubtedly take years), a court-ordered minimal flow continues to trickle past my shoes, delighting the dippers in search of aquatic bugs, the local osprey with a taste for fish, and the cottonwood seedlings that are beginning to take root along the bank. It is a fine spring day—a little raw, but invigorating.

It is particularly fine as there is some hope that Mono Lake will not indefinitely be forced to retreat from its banks, that the diversion rate of Rush Creek (and hopefully Lee Vining Creek) may be limited and the "bitter and fatal waters" allowed to recharge, that vertebrate and invertebrate life will be allowed to thrive—at least until the San Diego and Los Angeles city limits finally merge.

John Muir, perhaps looking from a vantage point similar to my camp on the slope beneath these craters, called this "a country of wonderful contrasts, hot deserts bounded by snow-laden mountains, cinder and ashes scattered on glacier-polished pavement, frost and fire working together in the making of beauty." He saw here things that we will never see—"rich oily windrows" of brine fly larvae driven up on the beach, "snow-crinkled aspens and berry bushes, growing on the banks of fine, dashing streams," Indians lying about their shoreline camps in "thoughtless contentment, their black shocks of hair perchance bedecked with red castileias, and their bent, bulky stomachs filled with no white man knows what." He speaks of bighorn sheep, sage grouse, pronghorn, none of which will be here again unless reintroduced and protected by the Forest Service as a program in their administration of the Mono Basin National Forest Scenic Area.

Diminished it most certainly is. But without its crown jewel, Mono Lake, it would be irredeemably diminished. It will take more time, more study to resolve the conflicts, but one hopes that those responsible for managing the basin's most precious resource will bear in mind that man is not only a creator and destroyer of environments, he is an integral part of what he creates and destroys. The piper may well take plastic these days, but the bill still comes in next month's mail.

3

The Lands Nobody Wanted

*I*T IS JUST AFTER NOON when I pick up my old traveling companions at the Reno airport—Bud Bogle, a furniture maker and river runner from Davenport, California, and George Wuerthner, photographer, former park ranger, former botanist with the BLM, former biology teacher, former student of mine, and formerly the inspiration for a jaunt around the Great Basin at its least appealing time of year—November. As they throw their gear in the truck I indulge in some advance whining about the cold, the rain, the wind, the lack of leaves on the cottonwood trees, the likelihood of snow. George insists the conditions are optimum. Although we are not going to get compulsive about boundaries, the BLM wilderness study areas (WSA) we plan to visit in Oregon, Idaho, Nevada, and Utah have never been the center of America's playgrounds under the best circumstances (largely because most of America doesn't know what it's missing), but in the late fall they should be completely void of the touring public. "Drive," he says. "Wake me when I get hungry."

And so I drive—from Reno to Fernley, past the Carson and Humboldt sinks and into Lovelock (named after the man who built the stage station there in 1862, not for the motel strip at the end of town), past the Rye Patch Reservoir with its few acres of Humboldt River water, on to Winnemucca. It is familiar turf to one born in Salt Lake City, half educated at the University of Colorado, addicted to Utah and Idaho rivers, and a resident of California. I have crossed the basin and range country so many times in half a century that I begin to recognize unravelled retreads in the ditches along the highway. I have never until now felt proprietary. But some of these empty miles (not nearly enough, I'm afraid) have lately been in the public eye as candidates for protected wilderness status, and I am suddenly curious to see what the stewards of the domain have chosen to include—and exclude. First I wake George to tell him he's hungry.

We leave Winnemucca after an early supper and head north on Highway 95 toward the Fort McDermitt Indian Reservation and the Oregon border. The barren ranges that lie between us and the Blackrock Desert to the west turn sulphurous in the last of the day's light, then fade to silhouettes against the evening sky. The sagebrush begins to lose definition as twilight settles into the basin, and the first jackrabbits begin to make their fatal, indecisive appearance beside the road. I reach to the dash to pull on the headlights. Along the horizon ahead there are answering winks from two oncoming vehicles, though how far away in this rarified, clarified atmosphere, how many dips and rises of this deceptively level plain, I have never learned to tell. The radio stations Bud has been fooling with in a doubtful attempt to get the first game of the World Series come from Grand Island, Nebraska, Everett, Washington, San Diego, California, sometimes all three at once, and we are reminded (if we needed any reminding) that desert country is designed to trick human perceptions in a lot more ways than the ubiquitous mirage.

At the junction of 290 there is a sign for Paradise Valley and campgrounds in the Humboldt National Forest. Bud and George begin to yawn suggestively, but I am full of Basque restaurant coffee and ignore them. Farther up the road the Fort McDermitt Indian Reservation is similarly marked with signs to tell us where we are and who's in charge. Nothing, however, has ever indicated that we have been traveling through hundreds of square miles of BLM land for most of the day. Public lands. Nothing to welcome us home here. No Dudley Do-Right standing at the entrance gate to take our three dollars and give us a brochure. In fact, since I descended the eastern slope of the Sierra and left the Toiyabe National Forest, there has been nothing to suggest we have been trucking about on our own eminent domain ever since we left the outskirts of Reno. One of the two most repeated questions asked by out-of-state travelers in the interior West must be "Who *owns* all this greasewood?" Followed, no doubt, by "What does anybody *do* in this godforsaken place?"

We'll ignore the rhetorical query, for now, finding its nonresidential bias suspect. To the first question let's observe that *we* own it. We the American people. Before our representatives in Washington began to carve up what remained of the nation's 2.3 billion acre landmass toward the end of the nineteenth century (after more than half of it had been sold off, deeded off, carted off), the public domain still amounted to well over a billion acres. But more of it was divested in land grants to individual states; some was given to the railroads, to canal companies, to the military; and some was pressed on the Indians we stole it from in the first place. We wisely saved a tiny bit in parks, monuments, and wildlife refuges, and "protected" about 191 million acres in forest reserves. And the rest—"the lands nobody wanted," as the saying goes—we eventually assigned to the Bureau of Land Management, an entity we created in 1946 out of two (now defunct) agencies in the Department of the Interior: the Grazing Service and the General Land Office. At the moment this amounts to about 174 million acres in the contiguous states, plus something over 100 million more in Alaska (the BLM is a little vague about its figures).

The Bureau of Land Management territory in the lower 48 is almost entirely in the West. There is a National Geographic Society map in the back of the truck that shows all this in symbolic color—dark green for forest reserves, light green for parks and monuments, gunmetal grey for military reservations, Wingate red for Indian reservations, cheat-grass yellow for the lands "nobody wanted." (Private property, one notes, is displayed in white.) Even when one knows all the statistics the map is still a staggering, prefrontal illustration of how much of the nation is federally owned—one third—and how much of that third is BLM land. We can hardly drive anywhere between the eastern face of the Rockies and the Pacific Ocean *without* passing through our own backyard.

It is a desert backyard, much of it, unless one includes

the 147.6 million acres of rivers, glaciers, arctic plains, forests, and mosquitoes in Alaska, almost all of which qualify as wilderness and none of which make it as a desert. The Naval Petroleum Reserve on the north slope of the Brooks Range may get less than five inches of rain a year, but because of the permafrost and low levels of evaporation, vegetation in the form of tundra thrives. And when one walks across that tundra, water squishes under the feet. The old growth stands of Brewer's spruce and Port Orford cedar in western Oregon's rain forests aren't desert either, as the spotted owls who live there will tell you. Neither is the King Range along the northern California coast. Rising abruptly from sandy beaches to summit peaks three and four thousand feet above the sea, it is forested by coastal chaparral and Douglas fir, and averages more than a hundred inches of rain a year. Decidedly not desert. The elk and moose and trumpeter swans (not to mention the occasional grizzly) who roam 74,000 acres of BLM territory on the Montana side of the Centennial Mountains have never heard of shadscale and pickleweed, though they would certainly recognize the paintbrush, columbine, cow parsnip, and aspen that spot the lush meadows beneath Sawtell Peak and Mount Jefferson. The lodgepole pine and Douglas fir growing in the Garnet Range between Helena and Missoula (site of the Elk Creek wilderness study area) do not thrive in an arid climate. Neither do the moss campion and mountain avens on the alpine tundra of Powderhorn Mountain, Red Mountain, and Handles Peak in the Colorado San Juans—wilderness study areas all.

The BLM logo, reflecting this diversity of terrain, is backdropped by snowcapped mountains from which a sky blue river flows past a towering evergreen tree. But it is pretty silent on the subject of deserts. Which is odd, because deserts are where its employees mostly hang out. And too bad, because deserts are where we are mostly heading when, shortly after dark, we cross over Blue Mountain Pass and down into southeastern Oregon. To the west the long escarpment of Steens Mountain, a major drainage for the Malheur Wildlife Refuge, spreads like a dark shadow against the star bright sky, and at odd places along our route vaporous mists rise like smoke from unseen creek beds crisscrossing the sagebrush plain. There is an October chill in the air, and I add heat to the lights and the ball game in the truck.

Past the tiny town of Rome, where the highway crosses the Owyhee River (currently a candidate for "wild and scenic" status), we pull off the road at a BLM ranger station where Wuerthner and Bogle burrow through the gear looking for ensolite and sleeping bags. I stretch the legs by walking down to the boat launch area above the bridge and stand for a while listening to the frogs and the swirl of silt-laden water as it slides past in the dark, remembering a put-in at this very spot almost a year and a half ago when four of us nearly bought the proverbial farm by running the river in a fifteen-foot Achilles raft at the highest flood stage in its recorded history. Normally a mild, bump-and-grind stream along its lower section, there had been a heavy snowfall in the Independence Mountains, followed by freak 80-degree weather, and all of a sudden flows that in April would normally measure six and seven thousand cubic feet per second (cfs) rose to the size and power of the Colorado as it drops through the vastly wider Grand Canyon. The waters crested at 24,000 cfs on the third day, and I remember the "wild" better than the "scenic" Owyhee.

It is not only the river that is under consideration for protected status, but a considerable amount of solid acreage elsewhere in Malheur County, and a total of 2.3 million acres in the state. And next door in Idaho another 1.9 million acres, and millions more in uninhabited, unimproved areas all over the western United States, for that matter—though one has to glumly note that the whole preservation process is at least a day late and a dollar short, and is being pursued with no great enthusiasm by the agencies charged with identifying suitable parcels. We wonder, as we hunker down into our sleeping bags, whether this trip to visit a few of these study areas will give us hope or break our hearts.

II

We breakfast in the little farming community of Jordan Valley, and then, at the edge of town where the pavement turns north toward Boise, we turn east on a dirt road leading through the Owyhee Mountains and into the Snake River canyons of southwestern Idaho. A high plateau called Juniper Mountain rises in the background before us, though we are still traveling through rolling desert tufted with Great Basin big sage, and creased by dry streambeds and stratified benches of Columbia Plateau basalt. Jordan Creek, flowing maybe 30 feet between its margins where we cross it, is lined with bare cottonwoods and the winter lavender of leafless willows, but it is easy to see that cattle have long had total access to the water in this area. The brush and grasses that would normally crowd the riparian zone have been grazed off and trampled into mud flats along both banks.

From a vantage point above the road where we climb to eat our lunch we can see Steens Mountain, almost a hundred miles to the west, rising above its shimmering base to a summit line that is clear as a knife-edge in this dry, unpolluted air. To the north the higher peaks in the Owyhees, some over eight thousand feet, are dusted with early snow. But for us it is still summer-hot in the afternoon sun, and we are grateful for the light breeze rustling the rabbit brush and fescue around our picnic. Wuerthner, a botanist by training (and occasionally by profession), begins a dissertation on the evils of cheat grass in North America and Bud settles back like a big yellow marmot for a nap against the warm rocks. Tiny mosquito-colored clouds drift into the sky from the south. My finger scratch idly in the soil beside me, eventually unearthing a small, rusty sign that says BLM WIL-DERNESS STUDY AREA. How it got up here I have no idea—the nearest WSA is a few miles to our east—but the bullet holes perforating its surface are a familiar indication of local sentiment toward the information it imparts. Maybe whoever shot it up carried it around in his pickup for a while before flinging it out where he thought it belonged. In the dirt.

What is this thing, then, this wilderness study area? The Wilderness Act was passed by Congress and signed into law by President Johnson on September 3, 1964. Which is a while back. Nevertheless, it was a major piece of conservation legislation, and in spite of its unfortunate compromises to a variety of non-preservationist interests, and its cumbersome, time-consuming, obstructionist regulations for getting any given area into a system of federally protected lands, it did, finally, give the Forest Service, the Fish and Wildlife Service, and the National

Park Service a clear directive to consider something other than exploitable economic resources in the management of their properties. Wilderness areas, the Congressional mandate said, "shall be administered . . . in such a manner as will leave them unimpaired for future use and enjoyment *as wilderness,* and so as to provide for the protection of these areas, [and] the preservation of their *wilderness* character" [italics mine]. In other words, no commercial uses in areas designated wilderness (exceptions, of course, for livestock grazing, ongoing mineral leasing, and ongoing mining), no building of roads, no building of structures, and no use of the internal combustion engine including outboard motors (exceptions, of course, for the odd motorcycle race, commercial rafting companies, scenic flights over the Grand Canyon, snowmobile touring, etc.—i.e., anyone who complains bitterly enough about the restrictions).

The BLM's authority to inventory and study appropriate portions of its territory for inclusion in a National Wilderness Preservation System (NWPS) did not come until 1976 when Congress passed the Federal Land Policy and Management Act (FLPMA). While the Wilderness Act established the criteria for evaluating public lands for wilderness status, and gave directions for management policy, it was FLPMA that set deadlines for recommendations and required that complete studies be conducted. No rush, of course, although during the ten years since the passage of FLPMA an inventory *has* been taken, and draft or final environmental impact statements actually completed on 704 of the 861 identified study areas—areas that total a measly 22,898,212 acres, out of which the agency finds only about 9.6 million suitable for inclusion in the system. With any luck it should spend the remainder of the twentieth century in court defending itself from 861 lawsuits.

We drive on through badly overgrazed country, native grasses like Great Basin wild rye and bluebunch wheatgrass having given way to a dense concentration of sage and an invasion of *Bromus tectorum,* also known as downy chess or cheat grass. It looks tasty, Lord knows, like a nice thick carpet of every bovine's favorite meal, but it is only a pernicious foreign weed. Aldo Leopold called it "ecological face powder" covering the ruined complexion of badly abused hills. When it is immature it serves well enough as second-rate forage; when it is mature its prickly awns cause sores in cattle's mouths, and they feed on it only when there is nothing better. Since it crowds out the indigenous grasses, and provides fabulous fuel for range fires that burn the browse that deer and elk and antelope (and sometimes a hungry steer) depend on for survival, there often *is* nothing better.

The road climbs into juniper forest as it snakes its way east into Idaho, and by the time we cross the summit and make camp beside a broad open meadow the sun has dropped and the air turned brisk. An aspen grove, rare in these parts, borders the meadow and provides us with downed limbs for our shameful campfire as well as shelter from a northwest wind. The trees in this grove are ancient, and there are no new saplings anywhere about to suggest regeneration. (The four-legged reason for this is right out there munching in the meadow.) In the arid West aspen seldom if ever regenerate from seeds. New growth is nothing more than sucker growth that comes up from old roots, and is most vigorous in the aftermath of fire or avalanche, but when fires are prevented (by man) and grazing animals repeatedly eat off the new sprouts, a grove (like this one) will eventually die of old age.

But there is hope. As we sit consuming huge platefuls of steaming spaghetti and watching an early moon crowd in on the twilight over the meadow, we see the slinking shadow of a dreaded killer emerge from the trees. He stops, lifts his nose, trots closer to the unsuspecting Herefords, crouches . . . trots closer . . . seems to be *bouncing* along, actually, not exactly *concealing* himself from his prey . . . they don't give him a sideways glance, come to think of it. Through the binoculars I watch him pass *underneath* the belly of a solemn old cow, zigzag between two calves, and generally cut right through the middle of the herd on his way to the far end of the clearing. So much for predation. He keeps his eye on us, however, and when Bud rises and picks up a branch to feed to the fire, he evaporates. Men with long objects in their hands are clearly no friend of the coyote in these parts.

Onward to Deep Creek, one of seven BLM wilderness study areas in Owyhee County (misleadingly combined under the singular title, "Jacks Creek Wilderness," in the agency's environmental impact statement). We have seen absolutely nobody since we left the Jordan Valley yesterday morning, and have not passed a vehicle except for a pickup truck lying upside down in a ditch somewhere near a south trending spur called Dickshooter Road. Finding no corpse in the cab we take a hike along a streambed marked on our topo map, "Hurry Back Creek." It appears to be fed by "Hurry Up Creek" and "Nip and Tuck Creek," though the significance of these activities to the waterless drainage we explore is not immediately apparent. The area is thick with curlleaf mountain mahogany, a sprawling evergreen with a rough barked trunk and a domed crown, growing larger on this plateau than any of us have elsewhere witnessed. I chew cautiously on a leathery leaf to see if I can ascertain what it is that makes this member of the rose family so attractive to deer and elk. "It's high in protein," George tells me, spoiling investigation.

Jacks Creek is excellent raptor habitat and for nearly twenty minutes a golden eagle has been circling us, tightening its gyrations in a kind of inverse conical helix until it is hovering almost directly overhead. Prospecting carrion? The white on the upper side of its tail feathers tells us that it is a young bird, less than four years old, but the sex of golden eagles is indistinguishable by any method other than a hands-on inspection. Which doesn't look like it's going to be possible. Deciding we're not dead yet it soars away across the Deep Creek gorge and disappears.

We are descending the eastern slope and approaching Grand View, Idaho. Juniper Mountain Road becomes Mud Flat Road, which turns into Poison Creek Cutoff, which ends near a Titan missile site on Missle [sic] Base Road just east of the Emigrant Trail and the Snake River. Not far, we note, from the Mountain Home Air Force Base Precision Bombing Range. Talk about reentry. Desertification is almost complete down here anyway, as we can plainly see from the pedestaling around the sagebrush. Might as *well* bomb it. Grazing has stripped the earth naked, except around the sage where animals can't forage, and erosion has left each shrub sitting up there on its little base like something out of Lewis Carroll.

We wonder about the longevity of the ranchers whose barns and corrals we have passed along this remote road. Severe degradation of the grasslands is obvious even to someone who knows little about range ecology, and there is nothing to suggest that anything can be done about it except to permanently withdraw these lands as habitat for cattle—an unlikely scenario here in the wild and woolly West (even though the wild and woolly West produces only two percent of the nation's supply of red meat). A lot of owners who work small spreads and lease their pasture from the government are living on borrowed time—living on federal props like range improvement subsidies and beef price supports, and by subleasing their underpriced government grazing permits to other ranchers for a substantial profit. If it seems heartless to wish they'd hurry up and go under, there is not a lot of time left for this country either, if it is to survive the plague of the cowboy and his cow.

III

Bureau of Land Management land has long endured a bad reputation with the touring public, in part because it has so often been characterized simply as desert—a sweeping and misleading classification, to say the least. Some of it, as we have noted, is *not* desert. In the lower 48 some of it is. Quite a lot of it, in fact, though "desert" is a generic term that seems to conjure up little more than sand dunes and Lawrence of Arabia to a lot of people who have never been there. Folks from southern California understand it to be a hot, boring ride between Los Angeles and the Las Vegas strip. My students at the University of California know it to be a hot, boring ride from Los Angeles to Las Vegas where Lawrence of Arabia is headlining at the Sands.

The problem with the generic designation is that it says nothing about altitude, latitude, longitude, drainage; it says nothing about wildlife, insects, avifauna, plant life; it says nothing about whether the animals who live on it (or in it) are grazers, browsers, scavengers, nest builders, burrowers; it says nothing about tar sands, uranium, coal deposits, oil and gas reserves. It does not say a thing for the rivers that meander across flatland or tumble through the carved rock. It does not distinguish between an alkaline basin, a shortgrass plain, or a slick-rock canyon. It can't tell a buzzard from a chicken hawk, an antelope from a jackrabbit, a bighorn sheep from a desert tortoise, a fringe-toed lizard from a pupfish, a cowboy from an environmentalist. Not even a hint in it of petroglyphs and pictographs and other relics of the Anasazi, known as the "people who have vanished." In short, it does not suggest anything about the multiple flavors desert comes in. Not much of a word. Sorry I brought it up.

At Wuerthner's suggestion we drive south from the Owyhees, past the canyon of the Bruneau and through the Duck Valley Indian Reservation into the Independence Mountains, where the headwaters of the Owyhee River now collect in a reservoir behind Wild Horse Dam. The shadscale, pickleweed, and four-winged salt brush of the Snake River plain give way to juniper-piñon woodlands and then subalpine fir as we climb to the summit of the Humboldt National Forest. The Jarbidge Wilderness, where three ecological provinces meet (Columbia Plateau, Basin and Range, and Northern Rocky Mountain), lies just to the east, its higher elevations already covered with snow.

Fifty years ago this was prime elk country, and until

recently the Nevada Department of Fish and Wildlife actually had a proposal on the boards to reintroduce these noble ungulates along this section of the Idaho/Nevada border—an audacious bit of foolishness that completely unhinged local ranchers. In spite of the fact that ranching contributes only 0.26 percent to the total income of the surrounding three counties, the Department promised to *shoot* the elk if there turned out to be any conflict with cattle production, but the local grazing board "gave commands" (to borrow a line from Browning), and with a little help from friends in the Nevada legislature, "all smiles ceased." End of the elk caper. The only elk around here now has an *o* appended to its tail (as in Elko) and is officially ranked Nevada's third mecca of gambling.

We motor through mecca as swiftly as possible, driving southeast some twenty miles to camp in Lamoille Canyon in the Ruby Mountains. I can remember as a child my family often passing this miserable spine of the East Humboldt Range on our way to Salt Lake and my father trying to pry me out of the comic books in order to get me to absorb something of the ambience of western geography. Years later my own bored and squirming son was similarly unmoved by a parental finger under *his* nose when it was *his* turn to peruse the inhospitable discoveries of Fremont, Joseph Walker, and Lieutenant Colonel E. J. Steptoe. The problem was that from the roadbed of old U.S. 40 the Ruby Mountains looked like desolation's angel and not worthy of all the fuss.

Wrong. More undeserved bad press. But the Rubys are under the jurisdiction of the Forest Service and therefore outside the purview of *this* tour bus. A pity, because the Lamoille and Thomas canyons, with their glacial cirques and U-shaped valleys, their jagged, serrated mountain ridges that rise nine and ten thousand feet high, their stands of aspen, mountain mahogany, whitebark and limber pine, their alpine lakes, are an astounding (and representative) contradiction to the lead-footed opinion that the entire Great Basin is nothing but a place to "put the hammer down."

It occurs to me, once we are out of the Rubys and back on BLM desert lands, that revulsion is an understandable position—for a highlander. Indefensible, however. Take Highway 93 south from Wells to Ely (as we are doing) and the ovewhelming impression is of one vast, ochered flat extending for hundreds of miles between transverse ranges of basaltic lava. But if you hang around long enough to let your eyeballs adapt—which is to say long enough for all that hammered, blasted, barren, awful, stifling strata to begin to look natural—you begin to notice subtle distinctions. Color, for instance. You begin to notice that the scrofulous quarter-section of sagebrush you just passed has great variations on a theme, and is obviously a lot more than just sagebrush. The straw-colored fringe along the road is bluestem wheat grass, the grey-green is indeed sage but the yellow-green is rabbit brush, and the olive greens over there on the rise are juniper and piñon. The black-olive is juniper, the martini-olive is piñon. Singleleaf piñon. *Pinus monophylla.* Stop the truck, George, we just passed a whole field of *Oryzopsis hymenoides.*

Also we have "Moonrise over Hernandez" happening right here between the Snake and the Schell Creek ranges. Down in the basin the sun has set, but it is still igniting the 13,000-foot top of Wheeler Peak, home of the second-oldest living organism on earth (the Great Basin bristlecone pine), and of the only living ice flow between the Sierra Nevada and the Rocky Mountains (the Matthes glacier). The moon, obviously on some schedule of its own, floats in the pink clouds above the mountain and turns Ansel Wuerthner to jelly as he tries to set up his tripod and get that black rag over his head before the whole image goes up in dusk.

IV

Two-thirds of the state of Utah is federal land, of which well over half (or twenty-two million acres) is administered by the BLM, 3.1 million acres of that in wilderness study areas—though environmentalist opinion holds that at least another two million should have been included. There is nothing, of course, to indicate this fact as we cross the Nevada border and wend our way southeast through the Snake Range and over the Wah Wah Mountains to Milford, Minersville, and Beaver. No signs welcoming us to the Public Domain, Land of Many Abuses. One would think the Forest Service and the National Park Service the only landlords who aren't embarrassed by their holdings—though considering the general condition of the properties they manage, they should be.

We cut over to the Sevier River through Buckskin Valley where the Old Spanish Trail found its way between the Tushar and Markagunt plateaus, then turn south again to Panguitch. Highway 12 joins Highway 89 at the mouth of Red Canyon, passes Bryce, drops down into the valley of the Paria, and climbs the northwesterly end of the Kaiparowits to a town that will be chiefly remembered in American history for having been second in line (to Kanab) to hang Robert Redford, conservationist, in effigy. Maybe they didn't like his movies; they particularly loathed his opinions on coal-fired power plants.

The BLM official who confronts *us* at the agency office in Escalante is amiable enough, though it seems true joviality is reserved for citizens wearing the fluorescent orange of the deer stalker. We are probably the only three people in Utah who are *not* hunters and who are *not* walking around looking like a popsicle (a distinction we may not live to brag about), but we buy more topo maps and pamphlets and guidebooks than the office has sold since summer tourist season and our host overrides his disinterest in having to converse with yet another bunch of tree huggers. Spoiling his day for a fact, we ask him for the latest news on the state's most visible and highly symbolic confrontation between developers and preservationists—a proposal to pave the Burr Trail over the Circle Cliffs and down the eastern side of the Waterpocket Fold to Del Webb's marina at Bullfrog Basin. Be a shame, we say, if the Burr Trail got paved. "Oh yes?" he says. "What's the difference? The way I see it, a road's a road."

Well, no. A dirt road is different from a gravel road, which is different from a paved road. There are two-lane roads, four-lane roads, six-lane roads. There are banked and graded roads, bridged and culverted roads. There are also roads that have none of the above—roads that follow streambeds, ford creeks, climb over talus slopes, get washed out, muddied, impassable at certain times of year. In short, there are roads you can drive your forty-foot motor home on (with your trail bikes and your boat trailer in tow) and roads you can't. The Burr Trail is one you can't—which is a major reason why the Escalante primitive area around Long Canyon, the Circle Cliffs, White Canyon, and the southern end of the Waterpocket Fold remains one of the most exquisite places on earth. But why quarrel? We came to pull up survey stakes, not argue.

A few miles north of town we leave the truck, shoulder a day pack, and follow the Escalante River due west toward Sand Creek and Death Hollow. High redwall cliffs mark the canyon on the south, and the river quietly winds along a broad, gravelly bottom speckled with sage, juniper, and piñon. Ubiquitous cottonwood lines the banks, but there are also abundant samples of Gambel oak, canyon maple, box elder, netleaf hackberry. The higher ground is a carpet of Indian rice grass concealing prickly pear and barrel cactus from the daydreaming hiker, and mormon tea pokes its phallic little stalks up between volcanic boulders that have washed all the way down from the Aquarius Plateau. Somehow Wuerthner, who leaps and bounds through all types of terrain like a now-you-see-him-now-you-don't dervish, manages to avoid puncturing himself on the *Cactacae,* but his shuffling companions are not so lucky. I sit in the shade of an overhang for nearly an hour, picking out spines that have nailed my Florsheim to my foot and wondering if the Kayenta Anasazi who lived here some eight hundred years ago ever had this problem.

Late in the afternoon a cold wind begins to blow down off the Escalante Mountains, and a storm gathers in the vicinity of Hell's Backbone. Retreating downriver toward the truck, we stop for a drink at a seep along a south-facing wall and pause, teeth aching from the startling coldness of the water, to look back up the canyon at an ecclesiastical display of sunlight striking through the holes between the clouds. The wind frees dead cotton-wood leaves, bright yellow with autumnal color, and flicks them like sparks against the blackness of the approaching sky. Unwilling to turn from this kodachrome spectacle, we stand transfixed until the first spatter of rain rattles off the cliff.

Transfixion becomes endemic as we wander this section of the Colorado Plateau, and while literary attempts to describe it become repetitive, its reality never ceases to astound. It is a reality with easy access. One doesn't need a guide, an outfitter, an internal frame backpack, a Moss tent, or lug soles on the bottoms of one's feet to see it. One needs only a jug of water and a peanut butter sandwich. A little curiosity helps, and a hat. The literal truth is (unfortunately) one doesn't even have to trek very far from one's car.

At the top of The Hogback between the town of Escalante and the tiny farming community of Boulder we sprawl on an outcropping below a stunted juniper and peel oranges for breakfast. The first light of day begins to brighten the desert below as we sit, munching, staring across hundreds of square miles of silent, cold, immensely empty, slickrock canyon. The Aquarius Plateau rises to form a 10,000-foot boundary to the north; to the south the sheer scarp of the Straight Cliffs drops to the floor of the Escalante River valley; to the east the triple barrier of the Circle Cliffs, the Waterpocket Fold, and the five peaks of the Henry Mountains hide beneath the glare of a rising sun. Deep in the canyon below the outcrop we can hear the muffled sound of Calf Creek Falls, white noise drifting up from a surrounding maze of fabulous, cross-bedded, multicolored erosion. Somewhere out there beyond the dun domes and the maroon mesas, the layered terraces, broken spires, Jurassic tide flats, a canyon wren practices his haunting scales against a shaded cliff deep in a sandstone gulch. Those clear, descending notes alone are reason enough to revere this vast wilderness, and to hope that through FLPMA and the Wilderness Act we can preserve it forever just as it is.

In spite of the obvious intention of Congress to save a reasonable amount of what little public domain remains unleased, undeveloped, and unexploited, both the Forest Service and the Bureau of Land Management have done everything in their power to subvert the intent of preservation legislation in all of its forms. They have illegally manipulated the process of inventorying land for wilderness study in order to eliminate areas of conflict with timber, mining, and energy interests (the subject, incidentally, of a 1985 House Subcommittee on Public Lands oversight hearing in reference to practices by the BLM in Utah). They have allowed roads to be built into areas under consideration (and interim protection) for wilderness designation (Wyoming's Red Desert, for example). They have issued oil and gas leases in critical habitats adjacent to national parks (Montana's Yellowstone, for example)—as well as *within* areas under consideration (and interim protection) for wilderness designation (California's Los Padres National Forest, for example). They have arbitrarily withdrawn wilderness study areas without public hearings when private interests have indicated a desire to develop the resources contained therein (Nevada's Calico Mountains, for example), and have attempted to justify their actions with specious excuses and cockeyed record-keeping. And so on and so on and so on.

The BLM lands that have been actually *designated* wilderness (as of January 1986) amount to a grand total of 368,281 acres, less than two-tenths of one percent of the total territory included within the National Wilderness Preservation System. And 366,281 of those acres were placed in protective custody by Congress through the passage of state wilderness acts, not through any initiative or proposal of the agency. The agency has recommended only 9.6 million acres as suitable for inclusion in the preservation system—in short, out of its entire 174-million-acre empire it finds that less than five percent meets the criteria to provide "opportunities for solitude or for primitive and unconfined recreation" and to contain unusual "geological, ecological, scientific, educational, scenic, or historical" values. Isn't that odd. From our vantage point along The Hogback we're looking at about three million acres of solitude in the Escalante alone. Just by turning in our tracks. And if this isn't geological, ecological, and *scenic* what is it?

"Wilderness is a resource that can shrink but not grow," Aldo Leopold once remarked, and went on to observe that it takes intellectual humility to understand the cultural value of nature unaltered and unimproved. Nobody ever accused a government agency of intellect *or* humility (or, for that matter, the capacity to manage land), but we have reached a point in our historical development when stale jokes about the "Forest Circus" and the "Bureau of Livestock and Mining" and the principles of "multiple abuse" and "sustained greed" no longer serve to mask bemusement with amusement. If we care at all, and many of us do, we can only be

stunned by the way our diminished patrimony continues to be frittered away. And angry. Angry enough to sit
right here with our jug and our peanut butter sandwich
and our monkey wrench until it is saved.

4

To Arizona and Busted

*H*OW MANY TIMES HAVE WE driven this road? How many river trips over the past ten years have washed us out somewhere in the vicinity of Four Corners, only to be confronted once again with the news that the quickest way west and home is south—south out of Utah to Page, Arizona and onto the Arizona strip through a slot in the Echo Cliffs above Lee's Ferry, across Navajo Bridge at Marble Canyon and along the foot of the Vermillion Cliffs, over the Kaibab Plateau to the little town of Fredonia, over the northern extension of the Kanab, Uinkaret and Shivwits plateaus toward the valley of the Virgin. Off the Arizona strip through a slot in the Hurricane Cliffs and accelerate madly on to St. George, Littlefield, Mesquite. On to Las Vegas and a different sort of strip. Out across the great Mojave to Quivira, Cibola, El Dorado. What, we always wonder, was the hurry?

This time it's going to be different, my wife insists.

We are going to stop. We are going to wander. We are going to peer into the "great arroyo" (as the first Spanish explorers called the Grand Canyon) from vantage points heretofore unvisited. Or at least *less* visited. Except for the highway described above, and a spur road across the Kaibab Plateau from Jacob Lake to Grand Canyon Lodge on the north rim, there isn't much pavement on the Arizona strip, which is to say, on any of that part of the state that lies north of the Colorado River. Bounded on the east by the Echo Cliffs and on the west by the Virgin Mountains, the area is in great part roadless, or traversed by dirt roads that often resemble a goat trail and are only sporadically marked. You guess where you want to go by the direction in which tracks disappear through the scrub and by a general understanding that the sun travels east to west. If you turn north you regain the highway. If you go south you eventually fall into that "horrid abyss."

Some of the strip is designated wilderness—which by definition is supposed to be roadless. 19,600 acres in the Beaver Dam Mountains, 36,300 acres of the Grand Wash Cliffs, 84,000 acres in the Paiute Wilderness, 7,900 acres around Mount Trumbull, 14,600 acres around Mount Logan, 110,000 acres of the Paria Canyon and Vermillion Cliffs, 6,500 acres in the Cottonwood Point section, 77,100 acres of Kanab Creek, 40,600 acres around Saddle Mountain. Included in the National Wilderness Preservation System by the passage of the Arizona Wilderness Act in 1984, the total area comprises about 397,300 acres—a drop in the bucket, actually—but fortunately, or perhaps unfortunately, it is hard to tell where the protected lands end and the unprotected begin. You can fool yourself into ignoring the threat to over 600,000 acres of this roadless region by proposed uranium mining. And there's nobody out there directing traffic.

Which is one of the reasons I'm amenable to a leisurely crossing. Another is that I have been browsing in Clarence Dutton's *Tertiary History of the Grand Canyon District,* and for the first time since John McPhee's *Basin and Range* I have actually enjoyed reading something about geomorphology. Dutton's study, in spite of its austere title and the fact that it is a U.S. Geological Survey report written in 1880 under the supervision of director John Wesley Powell, is an extraordinarily entertaining book. Dutton takes his reader along. As he examines the canyon district, he entertains, he gives his science lessons without forgetting that most of us are poor students and easily distracted, commands our attention with a power of descriptive narration that so exceeds our own meager scribblings we forget all this is about drainage and erosion, faulting and flexing, rainfall and declivity rate. "I have taken the liberty," Dutton writes, ". . . of attacking the reader through his imagination, and while trying to amuse his fancy with pictures of travel, have sought to thrust upon him unawares certain facts which I regard of importance . . ." He makes me want to go look at it all again, now that I have viewed it through his eyes and better learned how to see.

The five elongated plateaus that lie between the Virgin Mountains along the Nevada border and the Echo Cliffs near the western boundary of the Navajo Reservation comprise much of the territory Dutton's survey concentrated on during the summers of 1879–1880, territory through which we now travel as we turn off Highway 89 onto 89A and head across the Marble Canyon platform. The road winds down toward the river over a sloping desert of sage, rabbit brush, and Indian rice grass, and crosses the gorge a few miles below the confluence of the Paria and the Colorado at Lee's Ferry. The parking lot just across Navajo Bridge is empty except for a Winnebago and a Toyota pickup with a "cramper" on the back—the proprietor of which is having his picture taken in front of a monument to the old fugitive *cum* ferryboat operator, John D. Lee—"frontiersman, trailblazer, builder, a man of great faith, sound judgement, and indomitable courage." I wonder about the penultimate kudo on Lee's plaque, since John D. was the only Mormon ever tried and hanged for his part in the Mountain Meadows massacre near Cedar City, Utah. His judgment might have been sounder had he blazed a trail somewhat farther south of the crossing where he was eventually caught, and that now bears his name.

We stop to tie down a flapping tarp near the Hatch River Expeditions warehouse at Cliff Dwellers. Behind us, in the direction of Flagstaff and the San Francisco Peaks, House Rock Valley spreads out in a vast, undifferentiated plain of rocky washes and low, barren hillocks. Bracketed by the blue rim of the Kaibab Plateau on the west and the sheer wall of the Echo Cliff monocline on the east, it appears less than inviting, though it seems to have served well enough as winter range for cooperative livestock companies during the late nineteenth century, and still serves as home for one of Arizona's two buffalo herds. A Mormon pioneer, returning to Zion across this territory after a failed attempt to colonize a mission down on the Little Colorado, spoke eloquently of its hospitality when, on a rock at the spring near the head of the valley, he carved his name, "Joseph Adams," and the inscription "To Arizona and Busted on June 6 A.D. 1873."

In front of us the Paria Plateau terminates in the farthest extension of the Vermillion Cliffs, a one- to two-thousand-foot escarpment that stretches over a hundred miles from the southwestern end of the Markagunt Plateau in Utah to the Paria Valley. Powell called these walls "vermillion" because of the color they turn at sunset, but in the cloudless heat of this midday they seem washed out, the plication of their vertical surface flattened, and the distinctions between horizontal strata blurred to a uniform hue of pale rose. Dutton observed the phenomenon over a hundred years ago. Without the middle tones of light and shade, "the cliffs seem to wilt and droop as if retracting their grandeur to hide it from the merciless radiance of the sun whose very effulgence flouts them."

I join them in retraction when we pull over for lunch at a former campsite of the Dominguez-Escalante party, now an historical marker near the foot of the monoclinal flexure comprising the eastern front of the Kaibab. Lynn does what she can with limp lettuce, peanut butter, and a loaf of bread that resembles in color and texture the carboniferous rock on which we are parked. I sit muttering in the shade of the truck, pouring sweat, idly wondering what the good friars had for *their* lunch when, on returning to Santa Fe after a five-month counterclockwise circumnavigation of Utah's high plateaus, they stopped at this place in October of 1776 to open their picnic basket. Escalante remarked in his journal that the party had been rather discommoded by its recent diet of seeds and cactus fruit; Father Dominguez, indeed, had been flattened for several days by a terrible "pain in the rectum." Grumblers. I understand it was not all skittles and beer for the Franciscan explorers, but they fared better than many and, except for aspects of the cuisine, were treated well by the Utes and Paiutes they encountered along the way. While the route to the Pacific for which they had been searching did not pan out, they were the first Europeans to see the valley of the Virgin, the first to climb the Hurricane Cliffs and cross the Arizona strip, the first to ford the Colorado above the Grand Canyon (which they named), the first to map this country in detail and with remarkable accuracy.

Our map leads us four thousand feet up into the ponderosa forest of the Kaibab Plateau, and then (our first fatal mistake, for it is Memorial Day weekend) south from the junction at Jacob Lake toward the north rim of the Grand Canyon. The sage and rabbit brush and cactus of the Marble Platform give way to juniper/piñon and mountain mahogany, and finally to yellow pine, Engelman spruce, and aspen. We begin to flank a long series of grassy meadows where early wildflowers are beginning to spot the terrace with color and afternoon thunderheads are reflected in lagoons of winter melt. In less than an hour we have been transported from slickrock desert to alpine park. Indeed, by the time we reach the National Park boundary a few miles below Deer Lake we are caught in a freak snowstorm that forces us to the side of the road. Two hours ago I was hyperthermic; now I'm hypothermic.

Four out of the twelve chapters in the *Tertiary History of the Grand Canyon District* are written about the Kaibab and its unceremonious, southern termination in what

Major Powell alternately referred to as the "black depths" or "the most sublime spectacle on earth." Some of Dutton's most elegant prose is reserved for that particular moment on the densely forested plateau when, as he rides sedately across a meadow and through the pines, leaning from his saddle to pluck a wildflower from a shaded bank beside a stream, *dum, ditty dum, ditty . . .* "the earth suddenly sinks at our feet to illimitable depths. In an instant, in the twinkling of an eye, the awful scene is before us."

There are two awful scenes, actually. The first (as in *awe + ful*) derives from the incomprehensible chasm itself, from the power of one's emotional reverence for the majestic, from wonderment inspired by the ensemble of terraces, buttes, walls, amphitheaters, pilasters, gorges within gorges, that constitute the vision before one's eyes. One's ecstacy, it has been often noted, is tinged with a little fear. A little dread. There is nothing to say about all this, no way to articulate it—except to echo Dutton's own disclaimer, "Surely no imagination can construct out of its own material any picture having the remotest resemblance to the Grand Canyon." It is, as J. B. Priestley once remarked, a kind of landscape Judgement Day, ". . . not a show place, a beauty spot, but a revelation."

The second awful derives from a spectacle unavailable to Messrs. Powell, Dutton, Priestley, et al.—to wit, ten thousand tourists at Grand Canyon Lodge (one per vehicle) vamping the void with cocktails in hand, gawping from the terrace, the dining room, the bar, the cafeteria, hobbling down the Transept Trail, the Bright Angel Trail, the North Kaibab Trail, neoprene can-coolers in one hand, Nikons in the other . . . humanity in such an appalling, achromatic, featureless number that the moment we are reminded of our membership in this assembly we are suffused with a whole new fear, fear and loathing, and we flee the scene, screaming out the window of our own gas-guzzling four-by-four, "surely no imagination can construct out of its own material any picture having the remotest resemblance to Grand Canyon Lodge on Memorial Day weekend." Joseph Adams, you are not alone. To Arizona and Busted, May 25, A.D. 1987. It is not the Park Service's fault (except for allowing these accommodations in the first place). We need a national program of euthanasia.

It is long after sunset when we reach Pipe Springs at the northern end of the Kanab Plateau. Once the headquarters for various Mormon cattle cooperatives (whose wards had overgrazed most of the Arizona strip even by Dutton's time), later established as a national monument in 1924, it lies within the Kaibab Paiute Indian Reservation, and on this commemorative evening is stuffed with motor homes, all running generators to keep those televisions and air conditioners humming. No matter. We are headed in the opposite direction, down a dirt road that leads south across Antelope Valley and eventually into the Toroweap Valley, the lower end of which dumps in several abrupt descents nearly five thousand feet into the inner gorge of the Grand Canyon. I assure Lynn that we are not missing anything by crossing this part of the Kanab at night. She can take Dutton's word for it when he describes the Kanab as "a simple monotonous expanse, without a salient point to fix the attention, save one" (Kanab Creek). The Toroweap Valley, however, is a different box of rocks. I have seen the

Toroweap from the top and from the bottom—in fact from the bottom of a flipped raft at Lava Falls—and I would like to take this opportunity to stand on Vulcan's Throne, that volcanic cinder cone so representative of the basaltic nature of this region, and hurl a few selected insults at that rotten rapid down below. But somewhere in the dark, ignoring the carping voice in the adjacent seat reminding me that this is a leisure trip, that we could stop, that WE DON'T HAVE TO DO THIS MARATHON THING AGAIN, I make a wrong turn. "Just around the next bend," I go on insisting. "Almost there." But it isn't, and we aren't.

Eventually I relinquish the helm and we throw down in a sandy area strewn with prickly pear and agave. When we wake at 0600 after a brief and sullen sleep it appears we have somehow tacked quite far to windward of the Toroweap Valley—in fact, judging from the position of the volcanic peaks (platforms? buttes?) of Mount Trumbull and Mount Logan, the entire Uinkaret Plateau seems to have drifted to the east of us and we are lying in our sleeping bags looking back at the Hurricane Cliffs. To the best of my knowledge, which is negligible and, I am compelled to observe, utterly unassisted by any of the maps in my possession (no topo maps, of course—too easy to find one's way with topo maps), we are somewhere in the middle of a 250-square-mile section of the northwestern corner of Arizona, about twenty miles from Wolf Hole. Maybe. Wolf Hole is an address occasionally used by Edward Abbey (quite possibly as a joke); otherwise it is indistinguishable from the rest of the Shivwits Plateau—a broad, gullied plain of desert scrub rimmed by flat-topped hills, a nursery of great silence.

Even the literature dealing with the Arizona strip and the canyon district is quiet on the subject of the Shivwits. Dutton sidesteps a description of its geophysical features on the grounds that it resembles the Uinkaret, the facts about which he feels are more "compact, intelligible, and, on the whole, more complete." Other observers offer a line or two about its geological history ("the Shivwits Plateau is crowned by scattered volcanic cones"), or about its one bit of human history that seems to have captured attention—the killing of three members of the Powell expedition who had left the party at Separation rapid, climbed out of the canyon, and were discovered by an ill-tempered band of Shivwits Indians a few miles north of Mount Dellenbaugh. Powell's narrative itself devotes only about ten pages to that part of the river canyon that cuts through the Shivwits, and on the subject of the plateau above he has nothing to say other than to note evidence of its volcanic origins and to remark, "I know enough of the country to be certain that it is a desert of rock and sand . . ."

There is, to be sure, a lot of rock and sand. But there is more. There is unequalled solitude. We have not encountered a single soul since we turned off the pavement at Pipe Springs. There is magnificent, early light on the eastern face of the Virgin Mountains, in stark contrast to the dark and illegible slope across the valley from our camp. There is a pungent smell of sage and piñon and damp dust that triggers the memory of other wakings in other deserts. There is a walk I take down the wash (while Lynn works her magic on instant coffee, rye-crisp, and a wizened apple), and the astonishing color and multiplicity of wildflowers—yellow ragleaf, purple phlox, orange globemallow, red verbena, the white petals and egg-yoke center of prickly poppy. There is the strong, sweet perfume of lavender snapdragons called Palmer penstemon that I pick in a groveling gesture of atonement for last night's forced march. But the *bella dona*, I discover, has already provided her own bouquet of unmistakable intimation—white trumpet flowers of the sacred datura (nightshade) in an empty mayonnaise jar.

At a crossroad somewhere in Wolf Hole Valley we turn west into the afternoon sun and bump along toward Jacob's Well. The route descends a long gulch spotted with cholla and grizzly bear cactus, both in flower, then begins to climb through Lime Kiln Canyon toward the crest of the Virgin Mountains on the Nevada border. This is clearly not a habitat to visit in one's Beemer. Narrow and precipitous, rocks that have fallen from the palisades above us threaten to block the passage, and the old truck bed, burdened with its load of rafts and oar frames, bangs on the axle at every pothole and ledge.

We pull over for a moment near the top of our ascent to look back across the canyon in the direction of the Grand Wash Cliffs. A congregation of turkey vultures drifts in a clockwise eddy below us. The meridian sun shimmers off chocolate rocks, bleaches cross-bedded sandstones to the palest pink, washes the entire plateau in bluish haze. Distant buttes dance on mercurial vapors. Again the text is Dutton's: "There are no concrete notions founded in experience upon which a conception of these color effects and optical delusions can be constructed and made intelligible. A perpetual glamour envelops the landscape." Like staring into the void, it inspires awe—and a little dread.

Onward. At a turn just over the summit I encounter

a cow, who stares at me in brutish stupefaction before commencing a suicidal dash down the trail and out of sight around the next hairpin turn . . . where I encounter two cows. Then three. Soon I have a small herd, all of them stiff-tailed, bawling, befouling the roadbed in a beefwitted dash for sanctuary. Can't get distracted here. Must press on. Hope the rancher who owns this stampede doesn't see the dust cloud down there in Mesquite, out there on the great Mojave. Where the quickest way west is once again south, through that other strip, to Quivara, Cibola and El Dorado. I'm less sure than ever there is any cause for hurry.

Postscript

There is (of course) an environmental message that has been largely ignored in the preceding narrative. I have tried to resist the impulse to fire yet another salvo at the BLM and the Forest Service—since the lyrics are always the same—but I can't. The playback button is jammed. Two observations are therefore offered here as brief encore. Those who are weary can proceed straight to the lobby for intermission.

Since 1980, when what is believed to be the richest uranium deposit in the United States was discovered in Hack Canyon near the southwestern edge of the Kanab Plateau, 50,000 mining claims have been filed on approximately 1.25 million acres along the boundaries of Grand Canyon National Park. Most of these sites lie within the Arizona strip. In fact, according to our BLM custodians in the region, *all* of the Arizona strip that is not protected by park or wilderness status, or that has not been judged unsuitable for uranium prospecting because of the steepness of its terrain or the depth of its lava deposits, has been claimed. While only six mines are currently active in the canyon region (north and south rims), the potential for increased radionuclide pollution is frightening, to say the least. Every dump, every accidental spill, has but one river to contaminate.

Mining is the major threat to the environmental health of the canyon district, but it is by no means the *only* threat. Like every place else in the West, logging and livestock grazing are inexorably chewing up more and more of the public domain, and the Forest Service and the BLM are, as usual, facilitating the destruction with dogged determination. Take, for example, some of the fifty-year management goals defined in the 1986 Kaibab National Forest Plan. The Forest Service proposes to allow continued grazing at current levels of the 790,707 acres of listed rangelands *even though* it acknowledges that "Permitted grazing use [will exceed] grazing capacity in the first decade," and *even though* by its own minimal standards nearly forty percent of the range is in less than satisfactory condition. A reasonable observer might argue that the obvious way to restore deteriorated range is to give it a rest. The Forest Service, however, proposes to create *new* range by "treating" 24,645 acres of piñon-juniper forest—by which they mean "chaining"—by which they mean dragging a logging chain between two bulldozers and ripping up thirty-eight square miles of trees. The destruction of the piñon-juniper will provide more overgrazing lands for Arizona's welfare ranchers. And so it goes . . .

PART TWO

River Time

5

The Breaks of the Missouri

*B*OB SINGER IS A RETIRED high school band director. Now he runs river trips out of a sleepy little north-central Montana town called Fort Benton. There isn't much there any more since the reclamation dams that begin some three hundred miles east toward the North Dakota border delivered the coup de grace to a dwindling steamboat traffic, and the railroad that was proposed to run east-west along the Missouri got relocated to the north along the Milk. This is big sky country with a vengeance. Unbroken horizon. High plains grazing land. Ranches with people scattered few and far between. Fort Benton is their town trip when they don't want to drive all the way to Great Falls, forty miles away. It is also the outfitting point for the only remaining free-flowing section of America's longest and historically greatest river, the gateway to 160 miles of a wilderness virtually inaccessible except by foot or boat, the portal to a week of solitude in the last untouched, unaltered, unimproved stretch of the wide Missouri. And that is why we have come.

Singer not only runs river trips, but he rents canoes and equipment, and hauls people to and from the few ingress/egress points downstream. He is lean, wiry, weather creased, a human smokestack, a one-man historical society, and if he has an opinion about us five disheveled fools and our two thousand pounds of junk that he drops at Coal Banks Landing, a few miles below the Virgelle cable ferry, he doesn't express it. No doubt he's used to middle-aged hysteria at the prospect of great adventure; recycled Lewises and Clarks falling all over themselves to be off and away. He helps us unload the canoes from the van, admonishes two little girls trying to stone a rattlesnake that has taken refuge under their fisherman daddy's pickup, promises to meet us six days hence at the Kipp Park Bridge where Highway 191 crosses the Missouri on its way to Malta, and then leaves us to figure out how to get sleeping bags, tents, cooking gear, a week's grub (most of it in cans), and a few gallons of water into two seventeen-foot Grumman canoes.

My old friend and bowman on this expedition, Peter Nabokov, recalls that the ground on which we stand— (he sits, we stand)—was the site of Lewis and Clark's June 2, 1805 campsite, and as the heaviest of our supplies are being lugged down to the river he reads to us aloud from the journals which we have brought along. "Killed 6 Elk 2 buffale 2 Mule deer and a bear ... the bear was very near catching Drewyer; it also pursued Charbono who fired his gun in the air as he ran ... Drewyer finally killed it by a shot in the head; the (only) shot indeed that will conquer the farocity of those tremendious anamals."

"In the event you gentlemen have forgotten," says Nabokov, "Drouillard [nee Drewyer] was killed up at the Three Forks by some Blackfeet about four years after this incident. They scalped him."

By mid-afternoon we are loaded and still showing an inch of freeboard. We launch in windless, ninety-degree heat, and float side by side for a time while we share some cheese and rye-crisp and apples. Low bluffs drop steeply to the river along here, and above them the rolling prairie fades off in dun sage contrast to the green ribbon of cottonwoods and willows that screen the bank. In the shallow draws between the hills little bluestem and bunch grass and western wheat grass bow in a breath of hot wind, and are still again. Far to the south we can see the sharp etching of the Little Belt Mountains against the bowl of a cloudless sky. We are not far, my bowman informs me, his paddle comfortably tucked in along the gunwale, from the spot where Captain Lewis ascended from the river on June 13, 1805, and looked over what he described as "a most beatifull and level plain of great extent or at least 50 or sixty miles; in this there were infinitely more buffaloe than I had ever before witness at a view."

If we should follow Captain Lewis's example and climb out onto the flats, we ought to be able to see another outlier range to the northeast—the Bearpaws where Chief Joseph's Nez Percés were cornered on their fighting retreat toward Canada in 1877. As a boy on a Saskatchewan homestead during World War I, my father used to stare southward at the Bearpaws across fifty miles of withered grass, gopher mounds, and heat waves, and dream of cool streams. In the heat it does not seem worthwhile to climb out and return his look. In that direction the map is empty for at least a hundred miles, except for a string of little towns along the Milk River. Havre, the biggest of these, regularly competes with International Falls, Minnesota as the coldest spot in America. Today, we suspect, it might be one of the hottest. And we would see none of the buffalo that Captain Lewis saw. Neither would we see any of the Honyaker homesteads that Jim Hill promoted for the sake of his railroad at the turn of the century. The shacks have weathered and blown away, the fences are occasional leaning posts and scraps of rusted wire, the fields have gone to weeds and inferior range, and the antelope have reclaimed them. The antelope and the Indians. Up in that emptiness are the Rocky Boy and Fort Belknap reservations, poor farms contemptuously given back to the original owners when white men found them uninhabitable. Until oil or gas or coal or uranium is discovered there, Indian tenure is safe.

Reluctant explorers, we are made vicarious natives by history. We are not far from the place where, in 1864 or 1865, the Crow warriors Two Leggings and Sews His Guts surprised some Piegan warriors and paused on their journey to the trading post "on the upper reaches of Big River" (Fort Benton) to exchange hostilities. Two Leggings' account of his first coup (in a narrative edited by Nabokov and published by Thomas Crowell) tells of the Piegans firing their muzzle-loading rifles at the Crows and falling back to reload. "One hung behind and I shot him in the shoulder," says Mr. Two Leggings. "Reaching back, he jerked out the arrow, broke it, and threw it on the ground. He pulled out his knife and ran at me." Two Leggings shot him in the chest. That arrow, too, the uncooperative Piegan pulled out, broke, and threw on the ground. "I tried to keep out of his reach, yelling to get him excited. Then I shot a third arrow into his stomach. He made a growling sound, but after he broke that arrow he made signs for me to go back. I made signs that I was going to kill him. Then he made signs for me to come closer so he could fight with his knife, but I made signs that I would not." Since his enemy was nearly dead and there was no longer any reason to be cautious, Two Leggings dallied with him, shooting him a time or two for good measure, until finally the Piegan got the message and died while walking back toward his friends. "Then I scalped him and tied the hair to my bow."

Things are quieter along the Missouri now. I let the canoe drift with the current, trailing my paddle in the mocha-colored water. It is so rich with the silt of the unstable soils through which it flows, and so alkaline, that it is undrinkable, though after an hour in this late afternoon sun a hat full of it feels good on my smoldering pate. Our map, a revised and updated version of one originally published in 1893 by the Missouri River Commission, shows little change in the cut of the channel, little change, indeed, since the upper Missouri was diverted southward during the last glacial advance, and I am reminded once again that the topography before us is almost exactly the same now as it was when Lewis and Clark came through here a hundred and seventy-five years ago. When Karl Bodmer, the Swiss artist with Prince Maximilian's 1833 expedition, painted these walls and bluffs and spires, he painted them precisely as we see them now, though he had a habit of foreshortening his scenes.

It's difficult to imagine those first explorers on this

river. It's one thing to float *down* with a strong, albeit gentle, four-mile-an-hour current behind, but what must it have been like towing a fifty-five-foot keelboat that drew three feet of water *against* this current?—towing it in moccasins, and up to your waist in mud. In reference to the stretch of river we are about to enter, Lewis talks about obstructions so continuous that his men are much of the time up to their armpits in the water, and the mud "so tenacious that they are *unable* [italics mine] to wear their mockersons [spelling his], and in that situation draging the heavy burthen of a canoe and walking acasionally for several hundred yards over the sharp fragments of rocks which tumble from the clifts and garnish the borders of the river; in short their labour is incredibly painful and great, yet those faithful fellows bear it without a murmur." Just like Nabokov. Except that they had been at it for 2,300 miles.

We make our first camp a mile or two inside a section of the river called White Cliffs. The walls here, cut by centuries of flood and fabulously eroded by wind and storm, are nearly perpendicular and vary in height from two to three hundred feet. Composed of a soft sandstone, they have weathered into an architectural symphony of columns, spires, pedestals, flying buttresses, alcoves. Prince Maximilian in 1833 saw "pulpits, organs with their pipes, old ruins, fortresses, castles, churches with pointed towers." Meriwether Lewis in 1805 imagined "elegant ranges of lofty freestone buildings, having their parapets well stocked with statuary; collumns of various sculpture both grooved and plain . . . " Across from the low promontory above the river where we pitch the tent, the canyon rises nearly three hundred feet, and from the dark shadow in a split just below its escarpment the rock swallows which have nested there by the thousands flicker up into the twilight sky like bats out of the mouth of a cave. A flycatcher peers at me with evident curiosity from a dead cottonwood behind the tent, cocks its head and hops around the backside of a limb to peek at me again, upside down. And when I descend to the river on a sweep for firewood, a great Canada goose lifts out of the marsh grass at the edge of a gravel bar, soars across the water toward the sandstone cliffs, and then veers upstream, climbing steadily until it is lost in the aura of the setting sun. Night comes down with a pair of mourning doves softly calling from the trees below the camp.

We turn in early and I lie watching the night sky through the open tent flap, great thunderheads creeping up from the east on a full moon, monstrous anvils of silver-grey cloud, black-hearted and shot with lightning, beginning to pile up into a space so littered and bright with stars that even when the moon is finally eclipsed I can make out Nabokov, cocooned in his bag, snoring peacefully in the aftermath of his strenuous day. I roll on my back, thinking about the river, wild, virtually unmarked, missing only the roving bands of Minnetarees, Blackfoot, Assiniboines, the buffalo and the grizzly bear. Which is a lot, actually. The frontiersmen may have tamed this wilderness, made it safe for the likes of us, but at the same time they profoundly diminished it. That should be some kind of lesson.

II

Early the next day about a mile or so above Stonewall Creek where the river narrows through a steep-walled channel, we are swept into an eddy by the current and quite by accident spot a large nest high up on the cliff face with three or four downy fledglings peering down at us over their barricade of twigs and sticks. We nose the canoes into the shelf of mud at the base of the wall and clamber out, cameras at the ready, to try to find an avenue of ascent for close-ups. Let's ignore the suggestion that we float quietly by and not disturb the natives. Nabokov wants a shot from above, and he is halfway up a chimney he's found that will take him to the top when a big red-tailed hawk appears a hundred yards downriver, screeching like a banshee and swooping toward us as fast as her wings will propel her. In a matter of seconds her mate appears directly overhead, and together they circle the nest, shrieking their outrage and dive-bombing Stemplepeter, who changes his direction and his mind about baby hawks.

We proceed southeast with measured stroke, led, it seems, by two great blue herons who lift from their mud-shoal perch as we approach, flap a time or two, retract their ungainly legs, and settle into a long, graceful glide that carries them a quarter mile downstream where they wait for us to come loafing along. Mallards appear in the side channels. There are killdeer, tanagers, and a profusion of magpies in the brush along the cutbanks, and just before we stop for lunch we round the point of a low, treeless island and startle a pair of double-crested cormorants into flight. In real life I am not much of a watcher of birds, but their presence and variety in this wilderness is so insistent that even I cannot remain indifferent for long. I find myself paddling hard to catch up with the other canoe because its occupant, Bob

Lewis—no relation of Meriwether—is an ornithological encyclopedia, and he also has a bird book in his pack.

We stop again at the ruins of an old, stone-walled cabin, once a sheepherder's camp, no doubt, now a couple of standing walls with the axe-hewn window headers still intact and a pile of scree where winter snows have toppled in the rest. Rusted bedsprings and the remnants of a cookstove. Weeds and some small white flowers in the chinks between the mortared walls. Our map tells us that Maximilian and Bodmer camped close to this spot in the summer of 1833, and we walk the canoes down to a point that resembles one of our reproductions of the Swiss artist's paintings and sprawl on the bank, lunching on half a salami and some rye-not-so-crisp. A short nap; then back onto the river.

By late afternoon the country has opened up once more and the cliffs, though still steep and high, have fallen back from the main channel as much as half a mile, the sandstone now capped with a darker rock more resistant to weather so that isolated columns begin to appear that look like grandma's cookie plate, ceramic salt shakers, busted toadstools. The herons seem to like these as observation platforms. The wind has died and it is extremely hot. Nabokov confirms his growing reputation for careful and considered action by suddenly standing up in the bow and levitating himself over the starboard gunwale into the river. He emerges whooping and blowing with only his idiotic head visible above the turbid water, enjoins my idiotic son to follow, which nearly overturns the canoe, and I curse them sullenly for fifteen minutes until they begin to complain of the cold and whine to come back aboard. More bouyant than

they, I spin off with a flick of the paddle, and let them
float into camp.

III

Day three. Tang and oatmeal bars for breakfast, and
some salty words to cook Lewis about his expansive
cuisine. He wants an early departure, he says, because
we will stop tonight at the Judith, a long twenty-five
miles downriver. On May 29, 1805, after a hectic night
during which a bull buffalo ran full tilt through their
camp ("within a few inches of the heads of one range of
men as they lay sleeping"), Lewis and Clark came upon
a small but significant stream flowing into the Missouri
from the south, and Clark called it the "Judieths" after
his intended, Julia (Judy) Hancock of Virginia. They
found the campfires of 126 Indian lodges belonging to
the Atsina, allies of the Blackfeet—or so said "the Indian
woman with us" (Sacajawea) after she examined their
"mockerson" tracks in the sand. Ten miles upriver they
came upon a *pishkin,* a place where the Indians of the
upper Missouri, before they had wide access to the horse
and the rifle, used to drive great herds of buffalo over a
precipice. The most active and fleet young man of the
tribe would put on a skin with the head and horns still
intact and position himself so that when the hunters appeared he could pop up and run like mad toward a chosen cliff. The startled buffalo would blindly follow, the
decoy would try to time his arrival at the edge precisely,
drop into a pre-scouted crevasse just below the lip, and
let the herd thunder over to its death. Voila. The most
active and fleet young man became the toast of the te-
pee, the life of the evening party—unless, as sometimes

happened, he turned out not to be fleet *enough* and the thundering herd made a rug out of him.

Lewis remarks that the rotting carcasses they discovered "created a most horrid stench," and that the great many wolves they saw skulking around the neighborhood "were fat and extremely gentle." Clark killed one of them with a short pike called an espontoon, though Lewis does not say why. Probably for the same reason our mountain-man forebears killed everything—sometimes because they wanted to eat it, often just because it moved. In this respect little has changed, it seems, between the modern hunter and his historical counterpart. The expedition leaders, in consolation for their unappetizing find at the *pishkin,* apparently thought it proper to open the bar. Lewis reports that "notwithstanding the allowance of sperits we issued did not exceed ½ (jill) pr. man, several of [the men] were considerably effected by it; such is the effects of abstaining for some time from the uce of sperituous liquors; they were all very merry."

The upper Missouri below Great Falls is strictly a Class One river. We look hopefully at markings on our map like Pablo's Rapid and Dead Man Rapid, but they prove to be little more than riffles and a slight acceleration in the current. Just below the Slaughter River at the end of the White Cliffs we drift down on a flock of white pelicans bobbing in the water, much larger than the coastal variety I am used to, and possessing the greatest wingspan of any bird in this part of the country. We hold our paddles quiet and they watch us until we are within twenty or thirty yards, then lift laboriously off the surface and begin slowly to circle, gaining altitude an inch at a time like some jumbo jet corkscrewing its way out of a high altitude airport ringed by mountains. They are

snow-white with a fringe of black aeleron on the under-
side of their enormous wings, and the conical helix of
their upward spiral against the flat blue sky is completely
hypnotic. Around and around they wheel, now catching
a thermal updraft and rising faster, higher, higher, higher,
a speck of cosmic dust in a glinting bank around the sun,
still higher—until magically they vanish, absorbed into
the atmosphere.

I hear children swimming. The sound of their splash-
ing carries a mile up the river, destroying the midday
quiet, the contemplative float through the post-luncheon
nods, the illusion that we are alone in this wilderness
and protected from the babble of other anthropoids.
Somebody is swimming in *our* river. But nothing appears. The noise grows louder. We float down, almost
abreast. Still nothing. I stand cautiously and peer over a
low bar of cobble that forms the bank to my right, and
beyond it into a brackish-looking pond created by summer's recession in the flow of the river. What I see is the
glistening back of a dozen giant carp, their dorsal fins
and the scaly upper half of their goldfish bodies cutting
through the shallow water in a slow, almost meditative
glide, punctuated every now and then by a violent con-
vulsion that churns the water and produces the sound
we heard a way upriver. We beach the canoes and watch
them for over an hour, understanding finally the obvious
pattern to their ritual. Behind each female (and they appear to be about three feet long) swims a smaller male,
and it is he who thrashes the water with his tail to excite
the releasing of the eggs. The whole scene is so primeval
that we would stand gaping all afternoon if the wester-
ing arc of the sun didn't jog us on our way.

We camp at the Judith as planned. There is an old

ferry here, and a broad grassy bank along the river shaded by cottonwoods. A dirt road runs north for forty-four miles to the town of Big Sandy on Route 89, and south from the other side of the river about forty-nine miles to Hilger on Route 191 out of Lewistown, but neither is a road that anybody travels for pleasure, indeed for any reason except to get back to the ranch. A sign by the ferry says "Judith Landing Recreation Area," but I don't see anybody recreating except two fishermen setting trot lines for catfish and periodically emerging from their pickup to check on their luck.

It is hard to imagine this empty stretch of river ever changing, ever becoming a "recreation area" with all of the dubious implications of that designation. And not just because it was finally protected in 1976 when Congress, prodded by Senator Metcalf of Montana, placed 149 miles of it in the National Wild and Scenic Rivers System. It is exceeding remote to begin with. It is not the kind of country that stimulates most backpackers, has no white water to lure river runners, has limited access and primitive facilities at only a few places. Fishing is pretty much limited to goldeye, sauger, and catfish, and in a state full of blue-ribbon trout streams, who cares for that? If the BLM, charged with developing a river management plan, will leave it alone it might go unnoticed and survive. Or, if their plan includes banning the use of motors on boats, dynamiting huge craters in the primitive access roads, and allowing only ten people a month (for three months) to float down in non-aluminum canoes, gagged, and handcuffed to the thwarts, then it will certainly survive.

But it is a little worrisome when a government agency is asked to develop a management plan for anything, particularly when one considers what happened to the rest of the Missouri, the ninety-three percent under the direction of the Army Corps of Engineers and the Bureau of Reclamation. In the 1940s they came up with *two* plans for management—the Pick Plan, backed by the Corps, that stressed flood control and navigation, and the Sloan Plan, backed by the Bureau, that stressed irrigation and hydroelectric power. The two agencies fought so effectively for their pet projects that a frustrated Franklin Roosevelt decided to create a third agency, the Missouri Valley Authority, that would override the first two and get something accomplished. Then the Bureau and the Corps decided to cooperate; indeed, they decided to build *all* of the dams proposed by everybody. And that was the end of the Missouri River. The economic benefits from the watershed dams went mainly east, and the social costs were borne by the people of the regions through which the river flows—like, for instance, the Mandans, who lost much of their cultural history beneath the waters backed up by the Garrison Dam. So much for management.

IV

The fishermen are at their lines in the morning when I walk down to the river to splash water on my face. We exchange pleasantries. One goes back up to look after breakfast; I stand with the other admiring the view, letting the morning sun warm the bones and ease the stiffness from a night on the ground.

"You from these parts?" I ask.

"Born and raised," he says, baiting a hook. He has a

furze of Gabby Hayes whiskers and a roostertail of grey hair poking up where he slept on it. "My daddy came out to this country in 1890 and homesteaded a piece down on Hell Creek. Under water now. The Fort Peck dam flooded it."

"That's a real shame."

"Not much it ain't. I'd probably still be stuck there if it weren't for the dam." He ties his line to a short stick and jams it into the mud, throws the baited hook into the river, and we watch the current sweep it down. "Live over in Idaho now. The wife and I are just back to see her people in Lewiston, so Russell and me [he thumbs backward in the direction of his departed companion] came fishing."

"So, do you miss it any? This country, I mean."

"Oh, it's pretty nice country. But it's hard. I can remember before the war I used to work summers to get me a stake, buy myself a new rifle and some traps, and take off south along the river here to winter over. I could make a hundred dollars trapping for the season. In those days it was better than working for keep. Where you all from?"

"California." (I am sincerely hoping we won't have to go into it.) "What did your father do down there on Hell Creek?"

"Well, he raised horses mostly. He'd catch mustangs lost by the Indians or the cavalry and use them for breeding stock." I look attentive through the pause that follows and he opens up a little. "He had a line that was half Tennessee walker and half mustang that we called a Tennessee whip, because the way you broke it was with a whip. Only way to tame it was to beat hell out of it until you got its attention, and then I'll say it was a purty good horse . . . people prized it above any in these parts. But it was so goddarn mean it'd kill you if you didn't stay awake."

He brushes the sand off the seat of his pants and lowers himself onto a patch of grass, taking a can of Copenhagen out of his shirt and offering me a dip. "Whereabouts did you say in California?"

"Near San Francisco. Did you ever have one of those horses yourself?"

"No sir, I didn't but I was just a pip-squeak then. My daddy had one he'd whip-broke that he couldn't ever let it see both of his hands at the same time. If it only saw one it figured Daddy had his whip in the other and if it messed up it was gonna get coldcocked. But if it saw *both* hands, well, then it would try to stomp him for sure." He spits a few crumbs of snuff between his rubber boots and reaches down to pull in his line and remove a branch that has snagged in it. "I remember one old boy he hooked up with down there at Hell Creek, a trapper I think he was, and he had him one of those horses that had both its ears chewed off. That was how *he'd* learned it to pay respect."

From back in the cottonwoods I hear his companion holler to come and get it, but he is evidently a little deaf and makes no move to get up. "It was quite different, this country, back then," he says, folding his hands around one knee and rocking back. He appears to think about this for a while.

"Fewer people?"

"Oh my, no. Used to be all the land up the river to Fort Benton was homesteaded by folks who thought the railroad was going to come through. When they put it up along the Milk most just pulled out. Moved into towns.

Now that's another thing. Towns. Towns ruined this country. You know, it used to be that three or four sections would get together, three or four homesteads, and they'd hire a schoolteacher from Oklahoma or somewhere and set up a community school for the kids. Then the government started trying to consolidate everything into the towns, I don't know what for, and they began paying eight dollars a kid if their folks would transport them in to the town school." I hear his friend bellow that soup is *on*, damn it.

"That's when everything went haywire. Because, you see, if a rancher had four kids, why that was thirty-two dollars, which was enough for his wife and family to *move* to town and *rent* a place for the winter. Of course, the old man stayed out there on the place alone, and after a bit that got real lonesome, and the next thing you know he'd moved into town too, found something he could take up to do, and as often as not he never went back. It was easier in town. In my opinion, that's what ruined this country."

From the bank above, "Goddamn it William, you deaf old sucker, the flapjacks are gettin' cold. Fact they *are* cold."

"Well it's been nice talking to you," I say. "Good luck with the fishing."

William rises arthritically to his knees, then to his feet. "You enjoy the rest of your trip," he says. "It's purty nice country."

V

Below the Judith it is less nice. Or at least I think it not so interesting. Others who have written about this river have found the badlands along this eastern stretch more teeming with wildlife than the White Cliffs section, and the closer one gets to the Charles M. Russell National Wildlife Range, the more this ought to be so. Bighorn sheep and elk have been reintroduced in the area. There should be whitetail and mule deer in abundance, and this is the most likely area to spot a golden eagle. But we see, in fact, fewer birds, more signs of human habitation, and apart from a small herd of pronghorn antelope and a few beaver, not much along the banks. Captain William Clark, who more and more I am inclined to think was a distant relative of Machine-gun Kelly, suffered no such disappointment. He remarks in his journal entry for May 23, 1805, "I walked on shore and killed 4 deer & an Elk, & a beaver in the evening we killed a large fat Bear, which we unfortunately lost in the river . . . The after part of this day was worm & the Musquetors troublesome. Saw but five Buffalow a number of Elk & Deer & 5 bear & 2 antiloples to day . . ." The following morning, just to get his blood circulating, he "walked on shore and killed a female Ibi or big horn animal . . . in my absence Drewyer & Bratten killed two others . . ." A kill count from the Lewis and Clark journals might help explain our diminished sightings.

The weather begins to turn foul, with high winds and blustering rain squalls, and because we laid over a day at the Judith to swim and loaf we begin to feel pressed to make time. We aren't, but that doesn't seem to occur to anybody. Nabokov suggests we lash the canoes together and rig a sail out of a ground cloth and two paddles, and he and my son sit in the bow holding this contraption before the wind. No wonder we don't see any wildlife. We look like the last days of the Kon-Tiki, veering and yawing down the river, flapping like wash day at the asylum, but it works, and we rocket through thirty-five miles of twisting channel before we finally collapse at a place called Bullwhacker Coulee. Meriwether Lewis climbed out of the river here on May 26, 1805, a little over a year and two thousand miles from the day he and Clark and forty-three men began their trek to the Pacific, and he caught his first glimpse of what he thought were the Rocky Mountains, "covered with snow and the sun shone on it in such a manner as to give me the most plain and satisfactory view." His reaction to this discovery is all the more touching because he was actually looking at the Little Rockies of northern Montana rather than the great mountains he thought them to be. "I feel a secret pleasure in finding myself so near the head of the heretofore conceived boundless Missouri; but when I reflected on the difficulties which this snowey barrier would most probably throw in my way to the Pacific, and the sufferings and hardships of myself and party in them, it in some measure counterballanced the joy I had felt in the first moments in which I gazed on them; but as I have always held it a crime to anticipate evils I will believe it a good comfortable road untill I am compelled to believe differently."

I wonder what he would think of that road now? Take Interstate 15 to Helena and over the continental divide to Butte. Pick up Interstate 90 to Missoula, and then Highway 12 across Idaho and into Washington. You'll hit the Columbia just past Walla Walla and from there it's interstate again all the way to the ocean. Six months, you say? Now it's a two-day drive.

Rain continues to fall in windblown sheets, and we turn in at the first hint of dusk. In the morning we load the canoes and shove off in a gusting storm that turns the river to chop. Cow Island, where Chief Joseph and his band of Nez Percés crossed in September of 1877 (General Oliver Howard in hot pursuit) slips by to our left. In late summer and autumn when the river is low *this* was the headwaters of navigation for the steamboat traffic pointed west, and it was here that the supplies for the Royal Northwest Mounted Police were stored until they could be hauled by bull train up to the Canadian posts. The channel is much wider along here than it was above the Judith, the cliffs far back from the muddy banks, low and unremarkable. There are numerous side channels and grassy, treeless islands. Again, perhaps because of the weather, we see little in the way of animal life except cows and an occasional band of horses, and few birds except a crippled pelican, obviously the recipient of some idiot's shotgun blast, dragging itself along the beach at Tea Island, just before our pullout point at the Fred Robinson bridge.

Civilization. After the wildness of the upper river, the solitude, the illusion of being sequestered from humanity, returning to a world even as sparsely inhabited as northeastern Montana suddenly begins to seem like a bum idea. We begin to regret out loud that thirty-five-mile day when we did little but hunker behind an improvised sail. We should have spent more time *off* the river, hiking, poking around. We start to question one another about the infernal compulsion to log miles, check maps, figure out where we are and how far we have to go. Go where? To a steel and concrete bridge with cars zipping overhead, overflowing refuse cans, chemical johns, wounded birds? Pretty soon we aren't even speaking.

But it is only by contrast that this feels like civilization, and it seems extremely unlikely that this piece of the world is going to be much changed by the world's influx of tourists, developers, in-migrants, speculators, retirement communities, second-home owners, utility companies, or resort operators. There just isn't anything up here to make a buck on. Space and the wind in your ears. No thrills. For most people it is too hot in the summer, too cold in the winter, too austere in its emptiness, too far from port, too tough on the spirit. It will remain, one feels, the preserve of those who can accept it on its own terms.

6

Inland Passages:
Some Notes on Wild and
Scenic Rivers

O N AN AFTERNOON IN THE summer of 1981, three
hundred people gather at the amphitheater on the
south rim of the Grand Canyon, facing a handful of dig-
nitaries whose backs are to the abyss, and whose commemorative words are about to officially designate the
park a World Heritage Site—an honor then bestowed by
the United Nations on only six locations in the country.
A mile below the rim a tiny sliver of rusty water no bigger than a fingernail glints up in mute reminder of the
force that is responsible for this shocking panorama—
the Colorado River. The desert light is sharp as flint, the
day still and warm, the crowd hushed. A small band

trucked in for the occasion plays "America the Beautiful." Behind the speakers' heads a pair of indifferent hawks coast on the updraft from Bright Angel Canyon, glide laterally over the Tonto Plateau toward Indian Gardens, and disappear beneath the cliffs. And in the outback that protraction of geological time, that immense and unimaginable Grand Canyon of the Colorado, smolders in a pyrotechnic display of Coconino sandstone, Toroweap, Supai, Redwall limestone, and Bright Angel shale.

The Colorado River. Drainage for the entire western slope of the Rocky Mountains from the Wind Rivers to the San Juans. It is, as Philip Fradkin observes in *A River No More,* "the single most unifying geographical and political factor in the West." It is, as well, one of the most used, abused, controlled, apportioned, diverted, fought-over rivers in the United States. Except for an occasional flood, nothing has flowed from its mouth into the Gulf of California for twenty years.

An "irreplaceable resource," Assistant Secretary of the Interior, G. Ray Arnett, informs the audience as the ceremony proceeds. "Grand Canyon National Park personifies the Department's management philosophy to concentrate our energies to protect features of value to the entire nation and the world." As the old Eskimo in *Never Cry Wolf* says to the young biologist about to try out a diet of mice, "That's a good idea."

But let us not confuse a proposal with a policy. While we are being assured that features of value shall be protected, let us not forget the meaning of Lake Powell a few miles upstream. Let us not forget the 50,000 scenic aircraft flights that buzz Grand Canyon National

Park each year—or the whine of motor rigs down on the river. Let us not forget that the Bureau of Reclamation is busy rewinding generators up at Glen Canyon dam in order to produce more "peaking power"—more juice for the Phoenix housewife when she pops toast in the toaster and turns on *The Today Show* while Dad blow-dries his hair and Grandma pokes at the thermostat on the air conditioner. And let us not forget that back in Washington the bureaucrats are pushing a proposal to install additional generators in the dam's *spillways*. Let us not forget, in short, that the Department is proposing to further *deteriorate* the river corridor of the park it is dedicated to protect by creating even greater fluctuation in its daily flow. One stands in the heat of that August afternoon and wonders which "features of value" Mr. Arnett has in mind when he alludes to his employer's management philosophy—economic or aesthetic? His remarks illustrate both the problem and the paradox in the history of our nation's attitude toward its most essential resource—water—and toward the insensitive conduits that carry it from mountain to sea.

II

It has been 180 years since two American explorers pioneered a transcontinental route from the Mississippi to the Northwest—not exactly the inland passage sought by de Soto, Verrazano, Smith, Champlain and a host of other sixteenth- and seventeenth-century discoverers—but however circuitous and massively interrupted, a waterpath to the Pacific nevertheless. The prospect of fabulous trade with the Far East impelled the French, Spanish, and English; an imperial race to the Pacific and a trade war with the British helped motivate Thomas Jefferson to send his expeditionary force on the most important journey ever made on this continent. Economics, pure and simple. And Americans would continue to regard their waterways (not to mention the wilderness those waterways gave access to) in strictly economic terms for the next 150 years—first as highways for travel and commerce, then as a means of reclaiming arid lands, and finally as a source of hydroelectric power. Over the long run the process of hydro-development meant enormous changes in the richness of American life, but it came with a price.

Take any river as an example. Take the river we have just floated in our canoes. When Louis Joliet and Jacques Marquette discovered the mouth of the Missouri in 1673 during an exploratory float down the Mississippi, they were at once stunned by its size and power. "Sailing quietly in clear and calm water," Marquette recorded in his notes, "we heard the noise of a rapid, into which we were about to run. I have seen nothing more dreadful. An accumulation of large and entire trees, branches, and floating islands was issuing from the mouth. . . . So great was the agitation that the water was very muddy and could not become clear." But they were equally stunned, the record indicates, by its possibility. Might this, at last, be the legendary route to the Pacific? The river they were descending was clearly no passage to India, as they soon demonstrated, and while they had not actually ventured *up* this mighty side stream, the need to believe in a transcontinental waterway led Joliet to transfer his hopes to the Missouri.

The French explorers' wishful thinking confused geographical fact for the next 130 years, until Meriwether Lewis and William Clark set off up the Missouri on May 14, 1804 with a detachment of twenty-five men, a hunter, an interpreter and his wife (Sacajawea) and child, and a Negro slave named York. For the next twenty months they would travel by keelboat, pirogue, dugout, canoe, horse, and foot some 3,300 miles, from the mouth of one great river to the mouth of another, dispelling in the process over two hundred years of delusion and misinformation about inland passages, interior lakes whose waters discharged both east and west, mountain ranges of solid rock salt whose size was "known" to be 180 miles long by forty-five miles wide. It was not by following a single river, but a number of rivers—the Missouri, the Jefferson, the Clearwater, the Snake, the Columbia—that they would convert the dream of westward expansion into reality.

In time the Platte River Road would become the major highway to the Rockies; the Santa Fe Trail along the Arkansas would become far more commercially important. But the Missouri was the limb from which these branches later grew, and for two decades it was the main thoroughfare not only for the explosive fur trade but for miners heading into North Dakota, Montana, and Idaho and for settlers moving into the Northwest Territory. As late as 1887, when Jim Hill pushed his railroad west to Great Falls, the Big Muddy enjoyed a thriving steamboat business all the way from Saint Louis to its upper reaches at Fort Benton. It endured a rush of settlement from

Great Falls east toward the North Dakota line in antici-
pation of the railroad locating along its northern bank.
Honaker homesteads by the river. Most of them dried up
and blew away during a series of Montana droughts,
their owners already discouraged by Hill's decision to
lay his tracks farther north along the Milk. Economics,
in the form of land, brought them out; economics busted
them.

Economics busted the river too—at least that's how a
lot of people saw it. Reclamation, flood control, power.
Dams at Canyon Ferry, Garrison, Oahe, Big Bend, Fort
Randall, Gavins Point, Fort Peck. Bernard De Voto once
observed that "it is the forever recurrent lust to liquidate
the West that is so large a part of western history," and
sympathetic critics have pointed out that the Missouri
basin projects are a perfect example of a truth in action.
The people who lived along the Missouri suffered the
social and environmental consequences of "reclamation"; profits generated by the dams went east. And the
river, to use Philip Fradkin's phrase, was a river no more;
it was a waterway, a resource—dammed, diverted, apportioned. Only along 208 miles of its 2,700-mile
length—those miles from Fort Benton to Fort Peck—
does the Missouri resemble its once majestic, free-flowing past.

III

One could substitute almost any major river in this
brief and sketchy history. Give equal time to the Delaware and the Delaware River Compact, the Tennessee

and the Tennessee Valley Authority, the Columbia and the Columbia Basin Project, the Snake and the Minidoka and Boise Projects, the Sacramento and the Central Valley Project, the Colorado and the Colorado River Compact. This last, for example, divides the Colorado River into upper and lower basin states and allocates 7.5 million acre feet a year to each. [An acre foot is the amount of water it takes to flood one acre a foot deep.] A treaty with Mexico signed in 1944 guarantees it 1.5 million acre feet. By law the upper basin states (Wyoming, Colorado, Utah, New Mexico) must deliver water to the lower basin states (Arizona, California, Nevada) first, and then divide what remains according to their respective percentages. In theory this amounts to a division of 7.5 million acre feet, but in fact it does not because the river doesn't have that much water in it. Apportioned on the basis of an annual flow of 16.5 million acre feet (an abnormally wet year that has not been repeated since the signing of the Compact), the Colorado actually flows an average of 13.8 million acre feet per year. Because the upper basin states are required to deliver the entire lower basin allocation *regardless* of yearly fluctuations in total volume, obvious inequities are going to occur as individual states develop the capacity to use their entitlements.

The purpose in repeating all these dreary stats is to underscore the point that until very recently few people ever looked at a wild river, or a wild section of a tamed river, and concluded that the best thing to do with it was to leave it alone. The 1913 national debate over damming the Tuolumne in Yosemite's Hetch Hetchy Valley is an indication that early in the twentieth century there *were* a small number of people who questioned the need to "civilize" everything they could get to with a plow or a bulldozer, but the utilitarian argument prevailed, the dam went in, and the Hetch Hetchy went under. Not until 1956, when a coalition of conservationists led by Howard Zahniser of the Wilderness Society and David Brower of the Sierra Club defeated a Bureau of Reclamation proposal to install a dam at Echo Park, would preservationist opposition to a major water project prevail. The Sierra Club issued the first of its exhibition format books called *This is Dinosaur*, text by Wallace Stegner, clearly demonstrating that Echo Park would back the water of the Green River into Dinosaur National Monument, violating, as did Hetch Hetchy, the sanctity of land protected under the national park system. This time Congress said no.

Although the taste of victory soon included flavors of cinder and ash (the trade-off for Echo Park was Glen Canyon), the battle over Dinosaur signaled a gradual move away from the one-sided "use it or lose it" philosophy underlying national river management policy. In 1960, while the nine-year debate over the Wilderness Bill raged on, the National Park Service quietly proposed to the Senate Select Committee on National Water Resources that some of the nation's free-flowing rivers be preserved in their natural state. The committee agreed. The following year an Outdoor Recreation Review Commission report documented the need for a program of preservation, and the departments of Agriculture and the Interior began a joint study to compile a list of rivers (and river segments) that might reasonably qualify for inclusion. Of the 650 initially identified, 67 were designated for field studies and 22 were finally selected.

President Johnson added his endorsement in his 1965 State of the Union Address, saying that the time had come "to identify and preserve free-flowing stretches of our great scenic rivers before growth and development make the beauty of the unspoiled waterways only a memory." Then a three-year debate began.

The initial bill for a river protection act was introduced into the Senate by Frank Church of Idaho. As the floor manager for the Wilderness Act, he saw it as "patterned after, and intended to be a working partner to" that important piece of legislation, and he clearly understood that the 1960s had brought a change of mood on Capitol Hill—at least to the extent that Congress was willing to consider a few economic sacrifices in order to salvage a few remnants of the nation's undeveloped lands. Church relied on the Interior and Agriculture departments' recommendations for the rivers addressed in his bill and forgot, evidently, to consult with his colleagues concerning the inclusion (or noninclusion) of rivers in their respective states. He ran into momentary trouble. It was felt that "pork barrel" principles had always applied to water *development* projects; why shouldn't they apply to nondevelopment? Well, why not indeed. Opposition to that logic was scarce. And once everyone was assured that nobody's fiefdom would be encroached upon from outside, the bill passed without difficulty, 72 to 1.

But when the House Interior Committee received the Senate bill, its ranking member and most ardent conservationist, John Saylor of Pennsylvania, declared it "timorous" and "half-baked." Saylor wanted legislation that would place fifteen rivers in immediate preservation (as opposed to five proposed by Church), he wanted studies to begin on sixty-six others, and he wanted the authority granted the Federal Power Commission to license dam projects withdrawn from study rivers until Congress could act on them individually. Saylor's trouble came in the form of House Interior Committee Chairman Wayne Aspinall, one of the most formidable obstacles to preservation in the Eighty-ninth Congress. Aspinall didn't find a whole lot about saving wild rivers that interested him, and the bill died in committee.

Aspinall's indifference was not widely shared by his colleagues in the Ninetieth Congress. Several bills directed at river protection were considered, one of them the original Senate bill reintroduced by Church and amended in committee to include a number of the features of the Saylor bill, another a tepid little diversion introduced by the Colorado congressman himself. Aspinall knew that the sentiment for protectionism was high and perhaps felt that the best defense was a feeble offense. Discussions in the House Interior Committee took the better part of a year; Congressman Saylor finally introduced a compromise in July. It passed the House (267 to 7) as the National Wild and Scenic Rivers Act, and President Johnson signed it into law in October 1968.

In order to mollify points of view as varied as landowner groups objecting to condemnation authorization and insisting on the God-given right of American citizens to absolute control of private property, recreational activists arguing for boat ramps, campsites, and hot dog stands, and preservationists wanting no development of any kind at all, the act divided prospective waterways into three classifications—wild, scenic, and recreational. "Wild" refers to rivers that are unimpounded, unpolluted, inaccessible by road, and environmentally primitive (which no doubt accounts for their scarcity); "scenic" rivers may have limited, though inconspicuous, development and are accessible by road; "recreational" rivers are not only accessible by road but may have impoundments and considerable development along their banks. The critical point of the distinction, however, was how much development *would be allowed* once a river was included in the system—from none, to some, to quite a lot.

The passage of the act also placed parts of eight rivers in immediate protection—the middle forks of the Clearwater and the Salmon in Idaho, the middle fork of the Feather in California, segments of the Rio Grande in New Mexico, the Rogue in Oregon, the Saint Croix in Minnesota and Wisconsin, and the Wolf in Montana. Twenty-seven others (or segments of others—it was hard to find a whole river) were identified for potential designation and given interim refuge while studies regarding their suitability were completed.

But it was the protective language of the Wild and Scenic Rivers Act that constituted its most important feature—its prohibition of federally funded or licensed water projects, be they dams, diversion canals, dredging operations, etc., on any waterway in the system or under consideration. It said "hands off" to the Bureau of Reclamation and the Army Corps of Engineers and the Soil Conservation Service, and it forbade the Federal Power Commission (now the Federal Energy Regulatory Commission) from approving public or private hydroelectric projects, including transmission lines, within the designated areas. That is what it said *explicitly*. Implicitly it was a strong acknowledgement that the concept of biotic community extends beyond the *Hominidae,* and that "benefit" in a cost-benefit analysis should include not only flood control, irrigation, and power generation but the preservation of fish, wildlife habitat, archeological sites, and the intangible value of unmarred scenery.

IV

While the Wild and Scenic Rivers Act initially included only 789 miles of free-flowing water in seven states, it was the intent of the Ninetieth Congress that the total number of rivers included in the system rise to about one hundred by 1978 and two hundred by 1990. No such increase even remotely took place. By 1978, in fact, only sixteen rivers had been added to the original eight. By 1980, thanks to the enactment of the Alaska National Interest Lands Conservation Act that included wild and scenic designation, there were twenty-six segments of Alaskan rivers added. A subtotal of fifty. Add to this the Tuolumne in 1985, and eleven rivers that were not congressionally designated, but entered the system upon application by individual states to the Secretary of the Interior (an alternate method of inclusion provided for under Section 2(a)(ii)), and the current total comes to sixty-one. In seventeen years. Not much to crow about.

There are several reasons for *these* dreary stats—two in particular stand out. The inclusionary process is, to begin with, complicated and slow. Generally a local interest group will build a case for its favorite stream and convince its representative to introduce a study bill before Congress. Interior committees of both House and Senate hold hearings, complete with public testimony for and against, and, if the spirit is willing, report the bill to the full House and Senate for debate. If it isn't election year or impeachment year or approaching summer recess, the bill may actually pass and be sent on to the president for his signature. *Then* the Department of Agriculture or the Department of the Interior proceed to *study the river,* producing in time (generally a long time) a report that goes (along with an environmental impact statement and a draft management plan) *back* to Congress, the president, and the Office of Management and Budget. Then the whole process undertaken for the initial *study bill* is repeated—testimony, debate, vote, presidential signature. Five or six years may have passed since the local group first approached its representative (now deceased) before designation actually takes place. *If* it takes place. Congress can, of course, refuse to study the river, reject the study when completed, or do nothing at all. The third option has unfortunately become its general habit.

The cumbersome legislative steps prescribed by the Wild and Scenic Rivers Act are only partially responsible for the dismal record. Inertia and an indisposition toward its goals are probably more to blame. A river's qualification for inclusion in the system depends, in part, on one of those "features of value" concepts intoned by Mr. Arnett in his reference to the management philosophy for Grand Canyon National Park in the summer of 1981. The act declares it to be the policy of the United States "that certain selected rivers of the Nation, which, with their immediate environments, possess *outstandingly remarkable* [italics mine] scenic, recreational, geologic, fish and wildlife, historic, cultural, or other similar values, shall be preserved in free-flowing condition . . ." Yes, but who at the official level is making the judgment as to what constitutes this redundancy? G. Ray Arnett? James Watt? Donald Regan? Ronald Reagan? Whoever, the fact is that at the time of this writing only one significant addition to the Wild and Scenic system has been made since Reagan took office. His Interior and Agriculture departments have routinely delayed reports on study rivers, just as they have on wilderness study areas, and have attempted to have candidates rejected from final passage for no obvious reason other than the administration's anti-environmental bias.

The administration's river bill introduced in the Senate during the spring of 1983 by James McClure of Idaho is a case in point—sneaky, evasive, indifferent. On the face of it, it appeared to support the concept of preservation, proposing as it did to designate 245.2 miles of eight new rivers as wild and scenic. But that was all the good news in it. For no reason at all it chopped about 130 miles off the Forest Service recommendations for those rivers, and tacked on a couple of stunning amendments to the original Wild and Scenic Act itself—the first to delay protection for a designated river until three years after its inclusion in the system, thereby giving developers time to violate the intent of the law; the other to allow state legislatures by a simple resolution to *remove* rivers from the national system that had been included at the request of a governor and by approval of the Secretary of the Interior. Of the current sixty-two rivers, eleven could be deauthorized at the whim of a revolving assembly.

The conflict between those whose "features of value" include a large measure of unaltered and unimproved space and those whom Edward Abbey has described as boldly advocating the abolition of the last remnants of wilderness in the interest of industrial profit will not soon be resolved. Will not ever be resolved. It is built into our seesaw system, a system that houses under one institutional roof both dam builders and park rangers, a system that seems defined by paradox. Theodore Roosevelt stands on the rim of the Grand Canyon and says "Leave it as it is. You cannot improve on it. The ages have been at work on it, and man can only mar it." Theodore Roosevelt fathers the Reclamation Act of 1902 that creates the Reclamation Service that becomes the Bureau of Reclamation that proceeds to mar what the agency's creator held sacred. And would continue to mar if given its way.

The truth is the West does not need more water projects; it needs more efficient use of a finite resource, and a rational price structure that reflects the real value of that resource, and more free-flowing streams. The truth is the country no longer needs the Bureau of Reclamation's dogged pursuit of an assignment that made sense in 1902 but has been essentially completed. Over-completed. The truth is the Bureau has been an obsolete agency for thirty years. It should be congratulated for working itself out of a job and quietly put to sleep. Projects like increasing the capacity of megawatt output at Glen Canyon dam do not address the very real questions of limits; they are simply actions that accelerate us down the road to finitude. The conquest of a river, finally, is much like the conquest of the beaver who used to dam them. There is a point at which depletion turns victory into defeat, triumph into disaster.

Whether our grandsons and granddaughters, standing distractedly at some twenty-first century counterpart of a World Heritage dedication, will peer over the south rim into the Marble Canyon gorge and see a sliver of dancing river or a lifeless reservoir full of houseboats and water-skiers will depend on how doggedly we defend the principle that neither cost nor benefits can be strictly measured on a calculator, that wildness is critical to the human soul and must somewhere be accepted on its own terms. If we fail they may be attending not a celebration, but a requiem.

7

The Private River of Citizen Kane

THERE IS STILL SNOW ALONG the Forest Service road leading down into Fowler's Camp. Dean Munroe's truck
bounces over frozen ruts and the uncleared debris of
winter storms, and I ricochet off the side panels of the
bed trying to keep from being smashed by a levitating
pile of river-running gear—rafts, oars, rowing frames,
dry boxes. The morning air smells of pine pitch and hu-
mus, and as we drop lower into the canyon the damp
breath of riparian banks brings fern, willow, mossy rock.
Behind us, barely ten miles to the northwest, Mount
Shasta floats over the dark woodlands of Siskiyou
County like a Baskin-Robbins hallucination, a great
towering extravaganza of confectioner's sugar and
whipped cream, glazed with sunshine and topped by an
Aqua Velva day. Down below lies a stretch of river called
the upper McCloud.

What brings us to this remote spot near the Oregon border is both the search for new and little-used stretches of navigable white water, and curiosity about Munroe's increasingly publicized fight with the U.S. Forest Service over a permit to run the McCloud commercially. Munroe is the owner and operator of *Wilderness Adventures,* a guide service out of Redding, California, and his application to use the public facilities at Fowler's Camp and McCloud Lake as put-in and take-out points for the few trips he runs here each year has been denied—for no legitimate reason, he argues. And he intends to contest the matter all the way to court if he has to.

The dispute would not likely engender such media attention (even *USA Today* and the *Los Angeles Times* have done lengthy stories about it) were it not for its mythic proportions. A David-and-Goliath confrontation, one reporter called it: ". . . a commoner who dares to challenge the sovereignty of the ruler," wrote the *San Jose Mercury News.* Little Dean Munroe ("I lick the stamps, I buy the steaks, I row the raft") vs. a federal bureaucracy. Only the ruler here, it turns out, is not the Forest Service; it's the surrogate of Citizen Kane.

In 1920 William Randolph Hearst bought sixty thousand acres on the upper McCloud, virtually the entire seven miles of the still runnable portion except for the put-in and take-out, and he built a number of "castles" along its thickly wooded banks to house his family and guests during the odd summer retreat. Many of these buildings (collectively called Wyntoon) literally hang out over the river and are defenseless against the vulgarian hordes their owners imagine descending the McCloud should Munroe's petition succeed. According to the district ranger for the Shasta-Trinity National Forest, the

Hearst Corporation "just came unglued" at the prospect of gawkers in rubber duckies floating past their fiefdom. Hearst's Los Angeles attorney wrote Munroe, saying, "Your continued promotion of rafting the McCloud constitutes a direct willful interference with our client's quiet use and enjoyment of its property, which will not be tolerated." And the Forest Service, consistent in its history of accommodation to special interests, agreed with the Hearsts. Said District Ranger John Nelson, "The privacy issue is very important to the Hearst people. You can imagine their feelings if they had guests sleeping in one of those bedrooms on the river and twenty rafts came floating by. I guess I would be upset, too, if I owned the land."

I can imagine the feelings; I'm not moved by them. The Hearsts may own the land, but they don't own the river, even though they have had exclusive use of it for sixty years and would like to think they own it. Any stream that can be navigated in an oar-powered craft for even a part of the year is, according to law, a public waterway, and a lot of folks are inclined to think the public has as much right to its waterways as the Hearsts. Which is not to argue for unregulated use, or even, for that matter, commercial use. Whether individuals (or groups of individuals) should be allowed to profit from a public resource is an issue of some magnitude, but it has nothing to do with the Hearsts' opposition or the Forest Service's refusal to give Munroe a permit. "They just think I'll draw flies," he says. "People will hear about the river and come up, and they'll have to manage it whether they want to or not."

He may be more hopeful than realistic about those flies. Or so I think as we unload the boats and I stand there contemplating four hundred pounds of gear and what appears to be a two-hundred-foot vertical drop to the river. River? Peering down through the tops of the trees that grow along the bank, I observe what we used to call a *brook* back there in New England—narrow, rocky, a real bottom-ripper. Dip an oar in there and you lose the blade . . . or your teeth. "It's only like that for a mile and a half," says Munroe, "then you're in for a surprise." Actually I'll be surprised if I don't wrap before I ever *get* to the river.

We launch shortly after noon—Munroe's raft, mine, and four kayakers from Shasta City who are making their second trip in as many days. Without a stop it's only a three-hour run. The river descends at an average of forty-five feet per mile until it washes, seven miles downstream, into Lake McCloud, and then, Munroe remarks casually, there is an hour-and-a-half row on the lake before the take-out. This is not good news. To anyone who has rowed a white water raft on flat water this is very bad news. I'm beginning to think those flies look less ominous all the time.

For that first mile and a half I hardly have time to think about it. Munroe, whose boat is shorter and who knows the river well, has no problems, but I have all I can handle just keeping from hanging up in one boulder field after another. We narrowly avoid a logjam on one side of the river, get strained through a fallen tree on the other, bounce over a weir of submerged branches, and then, rounding a blind bend to the left . . . Munroe's surprise, the whole right bank of the river for 150 feet gushing with glacial runoff, subterranean plumbing from that albino mountain to the north suddenly bursting out along this cliff wall and cascading down into the McCloud, turning its water as blue as an ice cave, as clear as a sapphire. And tripling its volume, I'd guess. Maybe more. We're not talking the Missouri here, but we're definitely no longer on a brook.

The boulder gardens disappear beneath the increased flow, rapids build, and for the next two miles a continuous roil of white water keeps me so busy I have even less time to look around than before. The "crystal chute," Munroe calls it. The water isn't big (2+ on a scale of 6) but it is nonstop and cluttered with rocks. Every time I try to get a ferry angle to miss some upcoming fang I jam an oar in the cobbled bottom, blast it out of the oarlock, and punch myself in the mouth. This is no meandering pool-and-drop stream. No leisure time here to smoke, snack, sip a Bud, or attend to the bladder, Can't even slam down a Rondo, whatever that is. I think of Hearst's attorney and his letter, vehemently opposing any rafting activity "on the basis that the river is not navigable, that rafting will have a negative impact on the environment, that it will create significant risk of personal injury and encourage trespassing on private property." The first statement is demonstrably untrue, the second and third are highly speculative as well as untrue, and the fourth is bloody absurd. He must have been thinking of some L.A. freeway. Couldn't stop here to trespass if I wanted to, Randolph. No eddies, no beaches to pull up on, banks all choked with brush. There are a lot easier ways to storm a mess of castles than this. Of course, I *will* have a bit of a peek in those bedroom windows.

Around mile 4 things begin to calm down. A hawk floats overhead, a deer browses on the tender shoots of a budding alder, two Canadian geese explode off the water in front of the raft and veer downstream along the river corridor. We scan the treetops in hopes of spotting an eagle or an osprey. Then the flow carries us around a bend to the right and we are suddenly upon the real object of negative environmental impact—Wyntoon. A compound of five "chalets," the two that inspire the purplest prose are massive, three stories high and partially projected over the water, the pitch of their roofs broken by dormers, cupolas, spires, chimneys. The flanks of the central building are decorated from foundation to peak with life-size murals of fairy-tale characters. Architecturally difficult to define, all this. Romanesque Disney, perhaps, or Gothic Grimms. Medieval Maybeck. Tom Wolfe would know.

We drift past this apparition for all of a minute before it is lost to a bend in the river. No maidens in in the windows, no golden-haired damsel with her bowl of Nutri-Grain on the parapet, no squire in his knickers casting a royal coachman into the riffle below the wall. The place is empty, cold, and shuttered. Downstream we encounter a pagodalike structure in the Tibetan Tudor mode, a caretaker's house looking ordinary and out of place, and a sixteenth-century castlette with great arched windows and battlements. All that seems missing is Robin Hood and Little John and Friar Tuck. Hard to imagine the aesthetic sensibility responsible for this enchanted forest. And since we have not seen a solitary soul during this entire trip, it's hard to imagine whose privacy we have invaded. On our river.

Then suddenly we are out. The banks widen, the current weakens and dies, the oars grow heavier. If one doesn't mind rowing a 140-pound fat rubber sausage, the journey down the lake is pleasant enough; there is time, finally, to open the cooler and break out a sandwich and a soft drink. The only sound is the creak of the rowing frame and the dip of the oars, sounds that remind me I make these trips as much for this time of quiet as for the excitement of fast water. But I don't think the Hearst Corporation has much to fear—unfortunately. The upper McCloud canyon is pristine wilderness, but its access is difficult, its river-run too short to attract many who would have to come from any distance, its rapids too mild to attract the hard core. In fact if I ever do it again I think I'll sign on with Wilderness Adventures. Sit back and enjoy. Let Munroe buy the steaks and row the raft.

8

Deep Ecology

*T*HE STUDENTS IN THE BACK of the van think I'm nuts. For the past three hours I've been talking about nothing but the Navajo taco I'm going to consume at the Golden Sands in Kayenta, and to them a taco is a *Mexican* taco—a tortilla with meat and cheese and some jshredded lettuce in it, maybe some avocado. They have no curiosity about the Navajo taco, no gustatory memory of fry bread and beans. In point of fact they have very little curiosity about anything foreign to their subadult palates, their taste buds having been destroyed by tofu, alfalfa sprouts, yogurt, and herbal tea.

These students seem to evidence very little curiosity about anything at all. From Monterey Bay to Flagstaff, a distance of nearly nine hundred miles, they have lain supine on the floor of the van, sleeping, rummaging through my Conway Twitty, Merle Haggard, Charlie Pride, Melba Montgomery tapes (complaining), and occasionally dipping into private stocks of seeds and nuts.

One girl has eaten nothing for two days but garlic-flavored popcorn. The Mojave, beyond which few of them have ever been, holds no interest. One or two bestir themselves to look at the Colorado when we cross it, largely because they have read (or are supposed to have read) portions of Powell's *Exploration,* and because they've been lectured on the fact that this river is the major artery of the entire western drainage between the Sierra Nevada and the Rocky Mountains—a drainage, they dimly understand, that we will be floating when we put onto the San Juan River near Bluff, Utah.

"Looks dirty," the popcorn eater remarks.

The San Francisco peaks above Flagstaff inspire a yawn, as does the Painted Desert and the Little Colorado. Black Mesa, on the other hand, produces a communal outpouring of invective directed at Peabody Coal and Uncle Tomahawk Native Americans who conspire in the rape of Mother Earth. These students are, after all, majors in environmental studies, and while they take little interest in the actual environment, they are not short on opinions about its defilers.

We reach Kayenta about five o'clock, and I see Bud's truck parked in front of the Golden Sands, its trailer load of boats, rowing frames, oars, coolers, and miscellaneous gear in marked contrast to the more labor-oriented contents of the local Indian pickups. A patchwork of bondo and rust, it has once again earned its reputation as "the puker." I notice most of its human cargo sprawled in various angles of repose around the parking lot, exhaling carbon monoxide and trying to regain their stomachs.

My group, as usual, begins what is for them a laborious process of democratic resolution—will they eat or will they wait in the van?—but their need to hold a town meeting pursuant to action (any action) soon defeats me and I head for the restaurant alone. One of the remarkable things about this outfit, I mutter to myself, is that no one will commit to anything unless *everyone* commits.

Bud is inside concentrating on the purpose of our pit stop—the Navajo taco. The LARGE Navajo taco. A massive, mammoth, monstrous, Falstaffian, Brobdingnagian, Gargantuan, Cyclopean fatty of a taco served up on a plate the size of a turkey platter and weighing about twenty-five pounds. An acre of fry bread, a bushel of beans, a furlong of cheese, a firkin of lettuce . . . God knows what else. I can't see the top of his head behind the escarpment of his victuals, but I can hear heavy breathing and sybaritic moans.

The student consensus, apparently, is that it is too early for chow, and most have elected to cool their heels in the parking lot with the refugees from the puker. Four of the more adventurous ladies wander into the restaurant, through the melee of Kayenta Navajos, and sit sullenly at one of the few empty tables. I observe them shake their collective head when they are handed menus. Nothing to eat, thank you. We *will* have four glasses of water. The waitress regards them a moment without emotion. "You don't order, you don't sit," she says. They sigh, look put-upon, rise. As they make their way to the front and are about to exit, a young Indian with a walking cast on his left leg comes through the door. The popcorn eater nearly runs him down. "Excuse me," he says, lurching back. No response. She not only doesn't acknowledge his courtesy, she doesn't even notice him. He is vapor, wind, a figment of her imagination; he has to flatten himself against the wall to avoid getting knocked on his behind. "Excuse me again," he mutters.

Bud watches this cultural interface, slowly masticating the last wad of his fry bread and beans. "Maybe we better round up the wagons, Kemo Sabe," he says. "One of these dog soldiers is likely to give offense."

"*You* round up the wagons," I tell him. "I'll catch you in Mexican Hat. Because I'm gonna eat my taco, I don't care what."

Bud inspects the toothpicks in a shot glass on the table. "That's exactly what Custer said to Reno down there on the Little Big Horn," he says. "So *maybe* you'll catch me in Mexican Hat. Then again, maybe not."

Back on the road. Great thunderheads over in the direction of the San Juan Mountains, and rainsqualls streaking the sky around Mesa Verde. Or maybe it's just fallout from the Four Corners power plant. All around us the de Chelly sandstone buttes of Monument Valley are ablaze in the late afternoon sun. One of my wards is moved to crawl up off the floor and ask what makes them red. "Iron," I say. He wants to know how they got here in the first place. "Erosion," I tell him. Yesterday I might have been up to a more expansive discourse, might have bored him with the little information I possess about the intrusion of ancient seas and the deposition of sedimentary beds; about coral reefs and biothermal banks; about upwarping, downwarping, slumping; about river cutting, wind, spheroidal weathering, oxidization—nifty stuff like that. But this evening I just want to drive across the "rez" with my own head for company. I'm beginning to wonder if joining this expedition was such a good idea after all. I change my mind about these folks once we get to the river—rivers have been known to do strange things to my mind—but it doesn't look promising.

Who knows? It would seem that taking students who study the environment out of the classroom and into the "field" (I should say "down the river") ought to be an act of true pedagogical devotion. Either that or the greatest academic scam ever conceived—rafting on the taxpayer's dime, so to speak. Of course those of us who are merely serving here as "guides" don't have to concern ourselves with such hairsplitting—don't have to do anything, in fact, but drive the trucks and row the boats. Professor Pshaw, who should be waiting for us at the put-in at Sand Island, has done all the planning and outfitting. *He's* the one who will give the lectures and lead the hikes. He's the one who has to worry about one of these narcolepts doing a head-plant off a cliff (ground balls we used to call them at Search and Rescue). Drownings, broken bones, hyperthermia, PMS, snakebite, scorpions, fire ants, fire pants, impregnations, drug abuse—all his responsibility. The rest of us just have to keep this torpid, temperamental, hormonal mass moving in more or less the same direction—a chore, Bud has observed, rather like trying to direct a centipede through a maze, one leg at a time.

Dusk is upon us as we loop over the north end of the Raplee anticline a few miles southeast of Bluff. The great Comb Ridge monocline lies just in front of us, eighty miles of abrupt cliff face that marks the eastern boundary of the geological formation across which we have been bouncing for the past hour. The Monument

Upwarp, as it is called, is a kind of natural superdome, thirty-five miles wide and a hundred miles long, between the Colorado River on the west and the Paradox Salt and Blanding basins on the east. Its northern definition begins approximately at the confluence of the Green and Colorado rivers in Canyonlands National Park, Utah, and its southernmost extension is the Golden Sands Restaurant in Kayenta, Arizona. Well . . . near there, anyway.

Bisecting this wasteland of wrinkled rock and treacherous little thorny plants is the canyon of the San Juan (canyons, actually), cutting across the Grand Gulch Plateau, down through the Permian to the Pennsylvanian, exposing on its way a host of stratigraphic terms that basically describe time deposits of limestones, sandstones, shales, siltstones, marine organisms, layers of this and that—a kind of geological Navajo taco. I can never remember half the ingredients, much less the order of their spread. I can never remember whether the Cedar Mesa formation is on top of the Halgaito, or the Halgaito on top of the Hermosa. Or all of the above. Is it Moenkopi shale that caps the de Chelly sandstone, or Sinarump? And things like the simple distinction between, say, a syncline and an anticline just flat out elude me. I have to conjure the letter A (for "Anti") in my mind's eye and translate it to my finger, draw a diagram in the dashboard dust. The slopes meet at the top in a picture worth a thousand words.

But such details are of limited importance. I want you to sit up back there, you louts, and take notice. What is before you in this failing light is not scientific nomenclature; it is the most staggering image of cliffs, washes, canyons, buttes, mesas, towers, cathedrals, walls, potholes, draws, swells, folds, pockets, cones, spires, needles, and labyrinths, you're ever likely to see. Attention must be paid.

II

The San Juan River flows quietly between its banks at Sand Island, gurgling occasionally in the darkness when the subsurface current decides to boil up for a look-see. No telling what the river gods are doing out there. Once on the Rogue in Oregon I had one of those random boils suck down the rear tube of my raft before it decided to let go. But not on the San Juan. The San Juan is a gentle float without serious hydrolics. No rapids worthy of notice. Magnificent, towering walls, sandy beaches, hot sun and smooth rock, cottonwoods, the invader tamarisk, canyon wrens. The San Juan is distinctly a mellow experience . . .

"Except that we've got a problem," Bud says, coming out of the campfire light where he has been overseeing the preparation of supper and into the riverbank darkness where I have been hiding. He sits on a pile of life jackets unloaded earlier off the trucks and rolls a smoke. "We've got five vegetarians on board. They're caucusing right now about what they delicately describe as the 'nutritional inadequacy' of our commissary. They want to go into Blanding and buy tofu."

"*Tofu!* Blanding is thirty miles . . . and they're not going to find tofu in Blanding. *Tofu?*"

"I told them. They say they can't go five days without an acceptable source of protein."

"We've got all kinds of protein. Eggs, cheese, nuts, tunafish. What do they usually eat?"

"Tofu."

"Jesus."

We walk down to confront the congress gathered just outside the kitchen area where the other guides, Lynn and Don, are grilling burgers. Bud explains that going to Blanding is out of the question, and points to all the protein goodies we already have in the dry boxes—eggs, cheese, peanut butter, beans. "Those of you who don't eat meat can load up on beans tonight," he says. "We've got a huge pot going; you can eat bean-burgers, salad, fruit, cookies."

"We're not in the midst of civilization, folks," I add. "We'll just have to make do."

A girl named Chanterelle steps forward and eyes me malevolently. She is one of the smokers on the trip—she and a frail asthmatic kid everyone calls "Fuckin'-A-Fred," though the connection between this sobriquet and its object is opaque to say the least. Chanterelle, on the other hand, looks a lot like the mushroom she is named after—flat-headed and short-necked, shoulders like a nose tackle, no waist, no hips, no glutes. All stem from the armpits down. "What kind of beans *are* they?" she says, letting me know by her inflection that I am about to learn something.

"I don't know . . . beans are beans."

Chanterelle produces the empty #10 can and holds it up for inspection. "Have you read the label? *Ranch beans!*" she intones. "Cooked in *pork by-products.*"

Great God. Skewered. I can only shrug, walk away, hope everyone recognizes a Mexican standoff. "*Bad'ges? We don't need no stinking bad'ges.*" Anyway, this is Professor Pshaw's problem, not mine. I just drive the truck and row the boat. "Where *is* Pshaw?" I ask Bud. "In our hour of travail."

"At the Recapture Lodge in Bluff."

"Doing what?"

"Lodging. He said he's slept on the ground before. He said he'll be here in the morning to help load the boats."

The moon has come out. Same old moon, I imagine, that the Anasazi admired when they lived in these canyons as far back as two thousand years ago. They did all right on beans. A complete protein, the bean, when mixed with a little corn and squash. Freed the ancient ones from all that hunting and gathering and hitchhiking into Blanding for tofu. Gave them time to settle down a bit, take up the arts. In fact tomorrow we'll stop a few miles downriver to look at a whole wall of their art (petroglyphs carved into the Navajo sandstone at the mouth of Butler Wash), and to pick through a field of their pottery shards scattered around the base of the cliffs. Have to remember to tell the children to put everything back where they find it. It's wicked to steal samples.

There were at least three separate periods of Anasazi occupation in the San Juan drainage—roughly A.D. 200–400, 650–700, and 1050–1275. And then rather suddenly they left. *Why* they left is a matter of some speculation, but climate was probably the major factor. Tree ring counts and pollen studies in a number of granaries show a decrease in rainfall that reached serious proportions during the last quarter of the fourteenth century. Twenty-five years of drought coupled with a long-term population increase undoubtedly spawned a host of ancillary problems—overuse of depleted land, overirrigation, increased erosion, reduction of game animals,

reduced nutrition and a resultant susceptibility to disease—all that plus a growing paranoia that the guy in
the next gulch over might be plotting a raid on the food
cache. Whatever the specifics, by about 1300 they were
gone. And except for Fathers Escalante and Dominguez
in 1775, and a few trappers in the 1840s, nobody came
here again until the Corps of Topographical Engineers
under Captain J. N. Macomb in September of 1859. Macomb was not overly impressed. "I cannot conceive of a
more worthless and impracticable region," he said.

III

We commence our float around mid-morning. Lynn
and Bud will row the two bright yellow Domars, Don
the Avon Pro, I the old Achilles. We will each take three
passengers except Don, who gets the bonus extra—Professor Pshaw. The well-rested doctor makes his appearance at the last moment (looking badly hung over, to tell
the truth), but manages a brief discourse on the genesis
of "desert varnish" before dropping a wet beach towel
over his freckled pate and retiring to the shade of a cottonwood tree. The guides marshal the centipede into
the boats, give instructions about life jackets and sun-
stroke, and shove off. Rendered mute by the feeling of
release that comes with departure (all hype at last hy-
postatized) we slide quietly past low banks of gravelled
terrace and lean back at the oars to gaze on the flat-
topped mesas encircling the river valley around Bluff.
Boat bottoms scrape occasionally against submerged
spurs of mid-channel sandbars. The current wanders.
Seven miles to the west the river will slice through the

Comb Ridge monocline and speed up its twisted descent across the Monument Upwarp toward the Colorado, but here it is a slow meander, a good place to let the raft drift through lazy 360's. Work on the tan.

The students have decided to give themselves nicknames. As I float down on the Domars I hear passengers shouting back and forth across the water.

"Hey 'Shrooms, you got my #8?"

The unmistakable conformation previously known as Chanterelle rises from Bud's thwart tube. "What? Say again, Beaver?"

"My sunscreen. You got it?"

"Gave it to Warbler."

"Yo Warbles, 'Shrooms says you got my sunscreen. I need it, man, I'm turning the color of a crawdad."

"No way, Beav. Fuckin'-A had it at the put-in."

The boy called Beaver turns to the apparition next to him, something shrouded from hood to hoof in a white nylon rain poncho. Must be two hundred degrees in there. "Hey, dude, you got my #8?"

"Fuckin' A," says the wraith, poking it out through the arm hole of his tent.

Warbler? Beaver? 'Shrooms? The current catches my boat and carries me past the Domars. I look for expression beneath the baseball caps that Bud and Lynn wear low on their foreheads; see only the glint of river and sun in the lenses of their mirrored shades.

The great cliff of petroglyphs at Butler Wash is a howling success, less for the mystery of its symbolic representation than for the manner in which it has been defaced by modern scriveners recording names, dates, sweethearts, and hometowns in the soft surface of its ancient rock. There is also a spray-painted message across the length of the wall, "River Runners Go Home." Like the strip mine at Black Mesa, Butler Wash inspires outrage, as well as loudly expressed opinions about the disposition, percipience, and cultivation (not to mention lineage and pedigree) of the Caucasian geeks ("probably Mormons, probably from Moab") who carved these pitiful forgeries into the face of time. It seems pointless to brand oneself a racist by suggesting that the culprits are as likely young Navajo as Moabite whites—young Navajo who despise river runners (most of whom are white), and who have no reverence for the Anasazi either. The Anasazi are not the ancestors of the Navajo. Only the word is Navajo. Meaning "ancient enemies."

Interest in pot shards and geriatric graffiti terminates with the call for lunch. The discussion around the tuna salad (p.b.&j. for nonusers) turns to the Grateful Dead. Chanterelle and Warbler continue to demonstrate their contempt for the bill of fare and boycott the table, choosing instead to sit in a thicket of tamarisk and smoke clove cigarettes. I take my sandwich and walk up the talus slope below the wall to eat in the company of one of my favorite rock art characters—a little trapezoidal man (or woman) with a little trapezoidal head and little stick arms, legs, and fingers. Inside his trapezoidal head stands a still *littler* trapezoidal man (or woman)—with all the appropriate appendages. What is the meaning of this? What is that second fellow doing up there in that head? A mystery. Somebody once told me that the Navajo word for *soul,* directly translated, means "the one who stands within me," or "the one who guides me from within." Is that what we have here? Some Anasazi scratched a picture of his *soul* into the oxidized face of this ancient seabed? Totally far out! Intense . . . as the young persons say.

We make our first camp at mile 10 below the Mule Ear diatreme. Dr. Pshaw seems to have recovered from whatever ailed him at the put-in (the nap he took at mile 6 while the rest of us hiked to the cliff dwellings must have helped), and he steals a text from D. L. Baars's *Geology of the Canyons of the San Juan River*. Baars tells us (in Pshaw's voice) that the Mule Ear diatreme "is a kimberlite-bearing diatreme and contains a great variety of crystalline rocks from the Precambrian basement complex ranging from coarse-grained granite to gneiss to serpentinized talc-chlorite schist." Pay attention, scholars. There will be a quiz. "The presence of eclogite with dunite, pyroxenite, peridotite, and large blocks of kimberlite suggest that the separation of the gas phase took place at considerable depth, possibly near the crust-mantle boundary." Now . . . if there are no questions? . . . we are going to hike to the top of this volcanic vent to see if we can find any small red garnets lying around in its seventeen-hundred-million-year-old rubble. Look in the ant hills. The fire ant hills. Do not provoke the ants or they will make small red garnets on *you*.

As the students prepare for departure the vegetarian delegation approaches the kitchen. A swarthy, dark-haired boy now known as "T.V." (for turkey vulture) asks Bud what they can expect in the way of sustenance when they get back from the "dithyramb."

"Road-kill stew," Bud says.

"Sir?"

"An old river tradition. First night out we always have road-kill stew. Got real lucky at the junction of 89 and

160 and found us some prime, so tonight you get a choice—treaded veal cutlets or snake tiretire."

As it turns out, this is the last discussion we have about ingestion. Expulsion, on the other hand, is the subject of the evening performance—Bud and Don demonstrating the proper use of the w.c. (wilderness crapper), also referred to as the port-a-pot, or the groover. Regardless of its designation, its construction is always the same—a steel rocket can, double-lined with plastic garbage bags, and a removable toilet seat. Instruction is needed because (a) some people are shy, embarrassed, and revolted, (b) a *restrained* use of chlorox and lime disinfectants is required ("You are not baking bread," Bud always says; "do not flour the pan"), and (c) the groover accepts only solids. "Do not pee in it," Bud intones. "Pee in the river."

There would be little point in bringing this subject up had it not provoked our band of merry travelers into yet another attitudinal outburst. The chorus of boos verily echoes off the adjacent cliffs—*pee in the river . . . boo.* Bud remains calm, "Pee in the water, or in the damp sand beside the water, not in the groover. Everything we bring with us, we take with us—except liquid."

"*Boo. Polluter. Pig. Boo.*"

"The beaches are small and narrow, and the plant life is fragile. About six thousand people a year float this canyon, and if every one uses the area just around camp as a latrine, it becomes a very smelly affair indeed."

"*Swine. Litterbug. Don't listen to him. Boo.*"

"You better listen," Bud says. "Because if I find liquid in the groover, *you'll* find it in your morning coffee."

When the moon comes up I walk down to the beach

to check bowline knots and make sure everything is secure. Night winds have been known to whisk unfastened tarps, life jackets, clothing, even boats themselves into the river, and I have encountered some screamers in this canyon—night *and* day. At the Clay Hills take-out I once watched an unloaded sixteen-foot Avon picked up by a tremendous gust and blown like a leaf (or a barn door) for two hundred yards across the parking lot, flattening a half dozen rafters along the way, and taking out a loaded picnic table set up by a commercial outfitter for the delectation of his hungry customers. And more than once I have spent an irritable night sweltering in the bottom of my sleeping bag trying to avoid being sandblasted by a San Juan scirocco.

Don and Lynn are battening down the kitchen and discussing itinerary with Professor Pshaw—arguing a long river day tomorrow because we want to get at least to the entrance to the Goosenecks below Mexican Hat to camp. The students have retired to a tent ghetto they established before dinner, a circular arrangement with the opening of each hovel facing in toward the center. Bud is on his raft drinking a beer and trying, by flashlight, to unthread a nut off a bent thole pin. I sit on one of his tubes and dangle my feet in the water, looking up at the moonlit spine of the Lime Ridge anticline. "Why do you suppose they're all sleeping in a circle?"

Bud turns off the flashlight and stares out across the river—the grey-green, greasy Limpopo. "So that they can maintain constant audio/visual contact with each other," he says. "Part of the wilderness experience." He yawns, and tosses the thole pin in his repair kit. "You know, the thing about these folks that really gets to me is that they've got an attitude about everything. They don't *know* anything but what they've read in *Earth First!*, and they think that's all they need to back their self-righteous opinions."

"Sounds to me like you been quarreling with the clients again."

"Not quarreling, merely trying to instruct. I told T.V. to take the soap and wash before doing kitchen duty and he said he didn't use soap because it was made from animal fat."

"I hope you threw him in the drink."

"Actually, I just threw him out of the kitchen."

IV

Day two, and we need to make some river miles if we are going to get a decent place to camp tonight. Lieutenant Joseph C. Ives, who had about the same opinion of slickrock topography as his predecessor, Captain Macomb, commented on the paucity of decent places on the Colorado Plateau in his *Report upon the Colorado River of the West,* 1861. The area, he said, "is, of course, altogether valueless. It can be approached only from the south, and after entering it there is nothing to do but to leave. Ours has been the first, and will doubtless be the last, party of whites to visit this profitless locality." Wouldn't it be nice if that were so. Unfortunately there are a good many parties in this profitless locality right now, all hiking in the same side canyons, all vying for the best ground at night, all scowling at one another as they pass on the river. It used to be considered poor form to be *obviously* trying to out-row another trip to the primo campsite just around the bend, but now it is the norm. The BLM limits the number of groups that can launch on any given day through a lottery permit system, but the river still gets maximum usage and the old camaraderie that once defined an encounter between hominoids in the wilderness is a thing of the past. "Howdy" is an anachronism in the wilderness. Proprietary resentment is the fashion. "Who *are* those sonsabitches?"

So we log miles, while the students sprawl on the raft tubes and doze. The sun beats down, but there is a nice breeze that cools the sweat—and dupes the dreamer as he slowly dehydrates. Repeated warnings have been given about hyperthermia, but they have been received by our young hotspurs with the same attention paid all such instruction. "You ought to drink some water," I tell the people in my boat. "The desert is deceptive. Even when you think you're cool you're losing a lot of moisture." Patricia Clotworthy ("Cow Patty") raises her head and scowls, thereby exhausting her range of expression. The others sleep on.

Occasionally Professor Pshaw, riding in the lead boat, requests that we stop—twice for people to go into the bushes, once to inspect evidence of a fossil oil field called the Ismay algal biotherm ("See the leached oolites? That's the top of the Desert Creek cycle"), once at Mexican Hat Rock. There is a short trail to the base of the hat that the guides and four or five students run up. The rest of the party huddles in whatever shade is available along the bank. We make a fruit salad for lunch during this interlude, and when we're done Bud throws the residue in the river. Chanterelle regards him as if he just spat on the eucharist wafers. "The catfish and suckers will eat it," he says. "It's biodegradable."

"I wish you wouldn't do that anymore," she says, exhaling a cloud of cigarette smoke. "It's very offensive."

Twice during this layover I catch "the Beav" doing his business up behind the small sandy area where we have stopped. Twice I ask him not to do it again. He responds by briefly contemplating the rim of the canyon and walking away.

Our hopes for the good camp at mile 29 are dashed when we pull up on the beach under Mexican Hat Bridge to refill our five-gallon water jugs. The highway crosses the river here, and a short, rocky road down from the trading post above has been blasted out of the shale, making this a relatively quick and easy stop. It is even possible, with a little nerve, to drive down to the water's edge—indeed, two pickup trucks are parked at the far end now, two families of Navajo occupying an area next to the cottonwood trees. The kids frolic in the water, the women sit stolidly in the cab, the adult males hunch under the tailgate and stare out at the kids from under baseball caps that advertise the main reason they have come off the reservation. Budweiser. Coors. They are drunk. And they are not friendly. And when their kids start climbing on our rafts they call them sharply off. "Get away from those people. They got VD."

Under the circumstances it is, of course, impossible to keep *our* kids away from *their* (metaphoric) raft. It now becomes essential for the white brothers and sisters to demonstrate that they understand. The white brothers and sisters want to confirm the validity of the insult, and to assume full responsibility for the fact that the red brothers are wasted on a Tuesday afternoon, sitting in the dirt under a pickup truck with a six-pac and a brown bag and looking like they can't decide whether to puke, pass out, or go completely berserk. The white brothers and sisters would like to share the pain, the anguish, the all-consuming, uncompromising rage.

The Navajo, however, don't want to share anything. Including the same air. Custer's offspring are a familiar pain that can be either side-stepped, ignored, or swatted like a deerfly, but they're too dumb to be insulted. Insults seem merely to inspire them to higher levels of guilt. And now that they've got their quarry trapped at the end of the beach, they can't even be side-stepped or ignored. Perhaps they can be run over. *If they won't leave us alone, we'll leave them alone. Excuse me, again.*

As Bud and I are returning from the trading post with the water jugs we can see there's trouble down below. Evidently the Navajo have tried to depart by backing along the beach (no doubt at full throttle), and have been thwarted by Demon Rum and their own tempers. One of the pickups is half on its side, right rear wheel in the river and the other madly spinning a continuous plume of sand into the boats; the second pickup has a chain attached to the first and is creating its own grit storm as its tires scream and smoke on the loose shale of the ramp. A pale clutch of white brothers and sisters cringe behind the cottonwoods, confused, wanting to help but dimly aware, at last, that help is not wanted. The Indians are cursing as they try to avoid being decapitated by the shrapnel fired from under the tow, while at the same time they strain to keep the rear pickup from completely collapsing on its side. The truck drivers (now both women) seem to have but one purpose in mind—to mash the hammer to the floor until things either come unstuck or the engines blow. Bud sets his jerry can on the ground. "How do you feel about let's go get an eskimo pie?" he says. "Let things sort of work themselves out."

Except for the loss of the campsite caused by this minor delay we are not otherwise inconvenienced by our skirmish. The scene under the bridge seems to chasten the California cosmologists for a time, though there is heated discussion around the postprandial fire to the effect that the Native American predicament, as evidenced by the afternoon's events, is directly attributable to long-standing Bureau of Indian Affairs paternalism and a resultant confusion on the part of the Indian as to his status. This leads T.V. to a definition of Indian status. The Indian is the "first ecologist," he says. There is a collective murmur of affirmation. No one questions the absence of stitching in his segue. One brave lad named Wickham Snavely offers the unpopular opinion that Indians have been as guilty of clear-cutting, overgrazing, strip-mining, wasteful hunting and fishing practices, resort development, etc., etc., as anybody else, but his argument is spiked by Deadhead Darleen before it gets off the ground. "You're a racist, Wickham." Touché! Before long the circle around the fire tightens and Wickham, finding himself squeezed, goes off to bed. Thus we deal with the Pyrrhonist.

Day three, and we float through the Goosenecks, that curvilinear, meandering section of the San Juan that begins at the Mendenhall Loop and continues for thirty miles to John's Canyon, where things begin to run a little straighter, west-northwesterly, for another twenty-three miles to the take-out at Clay Hills crossing. The canyon is the deepest through this part, 1,235 feet deep at the foot of the Honaker Trail, where we spend an afternoon climbing the two and a half miles of switchbacks built in 1904 by a gold prospector named Henry Honaker. Some of us, anyway. Cow Patty and Deadhead Darleen are suffering from early symptoms of hyperthermia and have to be attended to by Lynn (all other concern simply eliciting tears and irritability). Others take one look at that monstrous, near-vertical wall of three-hundred-million-year-old sandstones, limestones, and shales, and decide to wash their hair. Wilderness exploration goes on the shelf when it comes to hair.

Too bad. Because from the top the view is unparalleled—the Abajos and the Henry mountains rise over 11,000 feet to the north; the snowcapped San Juans rise 13,000 and 14,000 feet to the east. Behind us Monument Valley spreads out in subtle shades of ocher, backdropped by the dark, looming mass of Navajo Mountain—which is backdropped in turn by a towering bank of thunderheads coming in from the west. And to our left, off in the direction of the Colorado River, lies the vast expanse of the Glen Canyon National Recreation Area, 1.2 million acres, decipherable in the late afternoon light only by shadow and horizon. We do not stand close to one another up here on this stone cap of the earth. We seek private spots for private thoughts, albeit private thoughts with a common base. Alone in the wind and rock it is perversely comforting to acknowledge, however briefly, one's utter chronometric and horologic insignificance. We don't matter, therefore *it* doesn't matter. Nothing matters. It takes a great load off. Relieves us of a great freight of pompous responsibility—before we dive back into our crack in the ground and return to the river.

Where our thoughts are less transcendental. Simple

matters prevail, like when to eat, where to sleep, where to set up the groover, who *are* those sonsabitches?—*they better not pull in here.* On the San Juan there are over three hundred campers stretched out along less than a hundred miles. Almost three people per mile. About five to six thousand each season. Outrageous. Given the circumstances, what is truly amazing is the relatively pristine quality of the riparian corridor. There is a reason for this, and it has nothing to do with an environmentally sensitive user public. It has to do with regulations that require the use of fire pans for campfires (and the removal of charcoal), bags or containers for carrying out all bottles, cans, and wet garbage, and the deployment of the portable pot. Why do the custodians of our national playgrounds not provide us with well-spaced, semipermanent, chemical johns, you ask? On some of the filthiest rivers in this country, they do. The problem is that many folks are called but few are chosen at the specific moment an outhouse floats by. The groover floats with you.

V

On the morning of our last day the sky emerges pale lavender above the cliff walls, unbroken and cheerless without sun. The night chill does not dissipate, and the students are slow getting up. I pull on my filthy old Patagonia jacket before crawling out of my bag, and squish down to the kitchen area on flip-flops that feel like two cold pieces of liver on my feet. Bud and Don already have the coffee going, and we stand with steaming mugs, staring stupidly at the river and listening to a canyon wren pipe crystal notes from somewhere in the rocks behind us. Gradually we achieve a functional level of consciousness and start to consider breakfast. Bud takes our big chili pot and a metal spoon and goes off to perform what has become his favorite chore—banging loudly and repeatedly in the center of the tent ghetto in order to rouse the inhabitants in as irritable a frame of mind as possible. Lynn appears, yawning, an "oh gosh, you're all up, shame on me" look on her face, grabs a cup of coffee, and disappears with her towel and toothbrush.

Don and I are cracking eggs when Bud returns with a look of deep disappointment. "Everybody's up," he says. "I don't understand it." He puts his pot and spoon on the kitchen box and waves irritably in the direction from whence he has come. Indeed, people are up. Not only up, but packing their gear before coming down to whine about the coffee. T.V., Cow Patty, and The Beav come up from the beach where they have been washing their hands. "Get outta here," they say to us. "We're kitchen crew this morning."

There is a lot of loud, angry shouting going on over by the tamarisk where three or four campers pitched their tents last night (the great circle of conjugates having apparently been disbanded). Pshaw, as usual, is still in the sack, and since we have been banned from the kitchen area by these uppity souchefs, the four of us drift over to see what the fuss is about. Chanterelle is berating Wickham for having smashed a scorpion with his shoe. He protests that it was crawling on his ground cloth and he didn't want to get stung. "It was out to get me," he says, in a fatal attempt at levity.

"This is totally anthropomorphic," Chanterelle tells him. "Totally. Why do you ascribe your own miserable aspirations to that harmless bug?"

"Because he was going to sting me," Wickham says. "And because he's not harmless."

"*He?*"

"Well, *it* . . ."

"You're not only racist, Wickham, you're sexist," Chanterelle says. "You're also an asshole."

It's good to see that some things are still normal this morning. "I hate to interrupt," I say, stepping forward, "but breakfast is about ready and we need your gear down on the beach before you eat. There isn't much current left and we're probably going to have to row most of the last five or six miles, so we need to move it."

Indeed, not far below our camp at Grand Gulch the current does give out. Lake Powell backs up the canyon of the San Juan nearly fifty miles from its confluence with the Colorado—that is to say, with the confluence of what *used* to be the Colorado, now a two-hundred-mile, stagnant, silt-laden reservoir behind Glen Canyon dam. What puddles up beneath us at this point is just the dead backwater of one of its torpid tentacles.

We pass the mouth of Oljeto Wash, flooded to the base of its first sandstone terrace. When the lake is low and the San Juan still a live river all the way to Clay Hills, this is the finest of camps—broad, sandy, protected—with one of the most enchanting hikes up through high, sweeping walls of Cedar Mesa sandstone. Today Oljeto is a shallow pond, a languid eddy with a Clorox bottle and a plastic plate slowly circumnavigating its perimeter. A half-mile below the wash Steer Gulch enters on the right, occupied by two boatloads of nudists who regard our passage with vacant disinterest.

Another mile, at Whirlwind Draw, I see Lynn's boat snubbed up to the rocks and Professor Pshaw wildly gesticulating from the shore. Both Bud and I hang up on sandbars trying to pull in, and Pshaw is beside himself when finally, towing ourselves with our bowlines through knee-deep quicksand, we reach the bank. "Hurry up, hurry up, hurry up," he keeps yelling. "We got an emergency. Chanterelle's down."

Down? Drown? What's he saying? We scramble over the rocks to a patch of sand where Chanterelle is indeed down, stretched out on a tarp in the shade with Lynn kneeling beside her, wiping her face with a damp cloth and talking to her in a quiet voice. The other passengers from the first boat hang around on the fringe, looking as if an alien had been discovered in their midst. "What's the problem?" Bud says. We can hear Pshaw back at the river's edge bellowing for Don's boat to "eddy out, eddy out."

"She got stung by a scorpion," Lynn says. "Apparently it crawled into one of the folds of her life jacket." Chanterelle moans that she's feeling faint, that her arm hurts, that she's cold, that she's burning up. "The problem is she says she's allergic to insect bites . . . bee stings anyway. But I don't know if this is a reaction to venom or histamine. I guess we could give her some Chlo-Amine and see what happens."

"We can give her a shot of Epinephrine," Bud says.

Pshaw is practically tearing out the remnants of his hair. "What is that, Epinephrine? Does that work on scorpions?"

"I don't know. Probably not."

"Well you're supposed to know. You're supposed to be a guide."

"I'll get the medical kit while you folks debate," I say, and jog back to the boat. Wickham is sitting on a rock holding my bow line, the faintest curvature of a smile gracing his lips. He looks at me without curiosity, but for some reason his disinterest seems manufactured. "Chanterelle got stung by a scorpion," I tell him.

"No kidding," he mutters.

When I get back with the kit Chanterelle already appears much better, and in fact is not going to suffer much more than a sore arm and a case of the woozies. Bud winks at me out of her line of sight and says, "I hope I remember how to stick a needle in. Only did this once before and that was to an orange."

"Naaoowwww," Chanterelle moans. "I don't wanna shot."

"Sure hope this doesn't induce cardiac arrythmia," Bud says.

"Forget it, Buster," Chanterelle tells him. "You're not going to use that needle on me."

"Looks like you're feeling better now, Chanterelle," Bud says. "Looks like a nice recovery."

But we wait for a while anyway, rocking on our heels in the cool shade of the cliff, until our patient's normally sour temperament begins to manifest itself in the suspicion that "that sonofabitch Wickham" might be responsible for her malaise. Recovery complete. Back to the river.

A faint roll of thunder booms up the canyon from off in the direction of the Kaiparowitz Plateau. The sky has turned dark and the air holds the smell of distant rain. Bud crawls across his rowing frame and jams his oars on the thole pins, anxious to get going before the wind comes up. For a moment he sits limply on his cooler, miming the wrist action of a dart thrower. "Actually," he says. "I bet there isn't a lot of difference between a mushroom and an orange. I bet it would have been the most fun I've had on this whole trip."

The rain comes down in sheets at the take-out, turning the clay banks where we unload the boats into a grease pit. "Slicker than snot on a doorknob," Chanterelle observes in her first approximation of humor. Maybe scorpion venom has a *non*-toxic effect on her. The California Cosmologists look forlornly at the trucks up on the rise as they trudge through knee deep gumbo with oars, frames, coolers, dry boxes, Bill's bags. A few revolt and head for high ground, but everybody else, amazingly, bends to the work without complaint. They are, in fact, so cooperative that once the gear is portaged they start to get in the way, and we have to prevail upon Pshaw to throw together whatever he can for a lunch and then load as many of them as will fit into his Volkswagen van and head back to Mexican Hat. From there they will go on to a Holiday Inn in Page, Arizona. Don volunteers to take the rest if we will load his raft and frame in one of the remaining rigs. Our pleasure, we assure him. We'll even clean off the mud.

When they are gone we pack gear into the trailer and Lynn's pickup, whistling while we work, stopping for a sandwich and a beer when the storm blows over. But we find there isn't much left worth eating. No tunafish, canned chicken, potted ham, lunch meats, Bac-o-Bits, pepperoni sticks. There's lots of wilted alfalfa sprouts, limp lettuce, and a few bruised tomatoes. Some avocados the consistency of guacamole. Some fruit. No cookies. We agree it just won't do. The herbivores have cleaned us out. There isn't even a can of ranch beans left to fill an omnivorous stomach. We need to get this junk loaded and hit the dusty trail—up the anticline, down the syncline, across the butte, over the mesa, through the potholes, washes, draws, swells, pockets, folds, gullies to the Golden Sands Restaurant where they offer up a gustatory memory. A great fatty of a gustatory memory. A LARGE gustatory memory.

Alone in the van I put on a Melba Montgomery tape and settle down for the long, slow drive back across the Upwarp to Mexican Hat and south through Monument Valley to Kayenta. The road over Cedar Mesa skirts the prologue to all the side canyons that dump into the San Juan from the north—Grand Gulch, Slickhorn, Johns—drops down into a corner of the Valley of the Gods to the river, then angles southwest across the Navajo reservation. A great pileup of afternoon clouds causes the light to slant sideways across the desert, illuminating a pinnacle here and a tower there, bringing a distant butte into sudden, radiant relief. Hail dumps on me as I cross onto the "rez" at the corner of the tribal park, but a mile down the road I am back in bright sunlight.

A Volkswagen van is pulled off to the side near Owl Rock. A dozen people with cameras blazing. Do I recognize this herd? I do. Darleen, Fred, Warbles, T.V., Chanterelle, the Beaver, Wickham, Pshaw. They have, of course, seen me. All waving madly. Better pull over. Might be something wrong with the Volks. Damn, a boatman's work is never done. They crowd around my van, pointing out rock formations, shafts of light, tattered hems of rainclouds, fork lightning on Navajo Mountain.

Intense. Far out. Totally nectar. Have I ever seen anything like it? Can I believe it? Is it too much, or what? *Outasight. Awesome. We don't want to leave.* I nod my head in assent. I agree with everything, with everybody. Cow Patty is actually smiling. Everybody is smiling. "Where was that Navajo taco place we stopped at before?" someone wants to know. Now *I'm* smiling. Pointing. Just up the road. "We'll follow you," they shout. All in unison. A democratic resolution, perhaps, but *right on.* Amazing how a wilderness outing can alter one's mind.

PART THREE

Outposts

9

Riverpigs and Yuppies

ALL THE WAY UP HIGHWAY 2 from Spokane to Sandpoint, Idaho, I keep passing neat little ranches behind pole fences, meadow grass springing up in the foreground like a manicured lawn, petunias blooming in porch planters, the raw earth of freshly turned gardens lying fat with seed. Along the roadside alders burst into lacy growth, a green salad against the dark backdrop of pine, fir, and hemlock, and while the mountains still hold a considerable snowpack, the tributaries flowing into the Pend Oreille River are littered with the flotsam of spring runoff. The traffic is light. Winter tourists who come to the Selkirk Range to ski Schweitzer Basin are gone. The summer visitors who fill Pend Oreille Lake with fishing lures and broken dreams of twenty-pound Kamloops have not yet come.

Driving along I realize I should have written for the 1905 Industrial Souvenir Edition of the *Northern Idaho News,* where uncontrolled boosterism led one local board to insist that in the creation of the Idaho Panhandle nature had distributed her "rarest gifts" with "wanton prodigality . . . withholding not a tithe of any of her graces that could possibly minister to the unfolding and development of the higher physical, mental, and spiritual qualities of mankind." These higher qualities, he claimed, were inspired by "larged-bosomed lakes, azure skies, mountains kneeling to the shores in an act of worship," and a climate "whose tonic effects create vigorous physical activity and the highest degree of mental nerve." Mercy.

Never, it seems, was there such a place as Bonner County. Early settlers had some difficulty deciding whether they were reminded more of southern Italy, Norway, Sweden, or Switzerland, but all agreed with our bard that "conditions of climatic equipoise realize in Idaho all the Utopias of nature which the fertile minds of idealists have created and wrapped in beautiful forms of poetry and prose." But the fertile mind of the above idealist referred only to northern Idaho, one assumes, since no self-respecting Panhandler would include anything south of Lewiston in his concept of Utopia. South of Lewiston one leaves the Pacific Northwest and enters Basin and Range country. Mormon country.

I myself have never been in this forty-by-sixty-mile slot between the borders of Washington and Montana, so my slow roll through the outskirts of Sandpoint, the only town of consequence north of Coeur d'Alene, is conducted without prejudice. I am not anticipating Norway or Sweden, and I am not much reminded of anything but a number of high, intermontane basins I know throughout the Rockies. The main difference is that Sandpoint is lower (2,086 feet), the surrounding mountains are heavily forested, and the open range one generally finds nestled beneath a ring of peaks is occupied by one of the largest freshwater lakes within the United States—forty-three miles long, six and one-half miles wide, 1,150 feet deep—a lake that on this day is as still and blue as a reflecting pool. Apart from one sullen thunderhead poking up behind the Cabinet Mountains in the Kaniksu National Forest to the northeast, the skies are indeed azure and the tonic effect of the snow-capped Selkirk Divide would have made Wordsworth's socks roll up and down. A less flippant metaphor might seem more appropriate, but coming upon Sandpoint inspires in me a child's glee. Hey, I tell myself, there *is* still a place unspoiled by hominids.

The town lies at the upper end of the lake where the Pend Oreille River flows north to the Canadian border and then west to its confluence with the Columbia. Before explorer and Northwest [Fur] Company partner David Thompson came down from the Kootenai River in 1809 and built a trading post on the eastern shore, the area was inhabited by Kalispel and Kutenai Indians, two relatively small tribes who lived by hunting, fishing, and root gathering, and whose amiable nature excluded them from much subsequent historical interest. At the end of the nineteenth century three major transcontinental railroad lines were constructed through Sandpoint—the Northern Pacific, the Great Northern, and the Spokane International—and with them came not only the region's single industry—timber—but a number of settlers who bought cut-over "stump ranches" at bargain prices from the lumber companies. Until recently if one wasn't a swamper, bucker, taildown man, riverpig, or some kind of small-scale sodbuster, there

wasn't a lot of excuse to be in Sandpoint. That is changing, but the limited economic base that prevailed until
the mid-1970s is perhaps why the town appears to me,
as I drive through it, still unspoiled.

Appears. Near the center of town I encounter a small,
dark cloud in the form of a natural food store, and
shortly thereafter a recycled bar now designated a crepe
restaurant. Homemade soup. Organic veggies. Next to
the C & L Saloon (country music every Friday and Saturday night) I come upon an enterprise announcing the
"Joy of Health. Natural Healing. Therapeutic Massage.
Reflexology." I begin to smell a California rat. I bet there
is a holistic center around the next block. I bet there is a
guy called Shalom Compost who treats disharmony
(formerly known as disease) with iridology and natu-
ropathic medicines (formerly water and allspice). I bet
his lady, Morning Meadow, is into shiatsu, and I bet their
half-wolf, half-Malamute dog wears a red bandana for a
collar. I bet they come from my own hometown on
Monterey Bay where a lot of that mischief was spawned
in the first place.

Well, let's move on. The lake limits the eastern and
southern boundaries of the town; the Selkirk Divide
rises four to five thousand feet from its backyard. Its
streets are heavily shaded by the trees they are named
after—alder, poplar, larch, fir, chestnut—and the houses
are modest, single-story structures for the most part,
clapboard or shingle, many with the metal roof one finds
in snow country. Except for the sparkling expanse of
water surrounding it on two sides, and the condo development sprouting along the beach at the tip of the
point, it could be any western mountain town, a little

neater, perhaps, a bit more "spic and span" because it depends increasingly on tourism for its livelihood, and because its residents seem to take some pride in the appearance of their lawns and gardens.

After a lunch stop for an otherwise respectable sandwich defiled by the ubiquitous alfalfa sprout (another West Coast invention, similar to atropine) I wander into the Bonner County Library and find myself in conversation with an elderly lady who seems to be the building's sole occupant. I ask her idly if she has seen much change in the town over the past ten years. She tells me, testily, yes. "The hippies moved in and ruined everything," she says.

The sprouts rumble ominously in my stomach. Hippies? So maybe Sandpoint *was* discovered by the modern Coxey's Army that marched to the hinterlands during the late '60s. "How did they manage that?" I ask.

"Why they're even living in the old schoolhouse in Hope where I learned my ABC's," she says. "Makes me mad, is what it does. My grandfather homesteaded up along the Pack River nearly a hundred years ago, my parents lived there all their lives, and I've lived here all *my* life, but those hippies think *they're* the homesteaders. Makes me sick, is what it does."

"I understand. Where do you think those hippies are coming from?"

"Well from *California*." Where else.

"Can't *all* come from California."

"It's what I hear."

Wicked California, everybody's root of all evil. Even mine. But maybe she is not that far off. Other people I talk with later estimate that fifty percent of Sandpoint's population is recent in-migrants from the West Coast, though nobody seems sure what that means in precise numbers. The old sign on the way into town says Pop. 4,460, but there is more like twice that number within the city limits, and four or five times that many in the immediate environs. Still, that's a lot of hippies.

The truth is I don't see much evidence of a hippie invasion, though I'm willing to believe it took place—to some extent. A lot of experiments in alternative lifestyles died rather quickly after the romance of rural America was actually experienced—and the first hard winter came down. And a good many more got pretty conventional as their adherents acquired some grey hair and a taste for a few of the amenities. I see none of the "street people" so common up and down the Pacific Coast, a phylum still *called* hippies, but fundamentally different because composed of a transient subculture devoid of any ideology, direction, or credo beyond the immediate gratification of vague cravings—at anybody's expense but their own. Sort of like the timber and mining industry, come to think of it. The lady in the library is using a label that symbolizes for her *all* change in the status quo, and particularly changes in community values that come with *any* urban in-migration.

We change the subject, chat for a moment about recent hardships in the lumber business, and then as I'm leaving she says, "I hope you aren't going to write about the drug issue."

"I didn't know there was one," I say, wondering how she pegged me for a writer.

"There isn't. It's been greatly exaggerated."

"Well I'm more interested in demographics than

drugs," I assure her, not bothering to observe that drugs and demographics go hand in hand.

"That's good," she says. "Nobody needs to hear any more about that business."

I wave and head for the door.

"Have a good one," she says.

II

It doesn't take a Charles Kuralt to learn that Sandpoint is no different from any other outpost of Eden recently discovered by people looking for a mellower way of life—no different from, say, Aspen (which it aspires to emulate) or Santa Fe, Taos, Mendocino, the San Juans, Bend, Boulder, Telluride, Sedona, Santa Cruz. It is only less far along its way than many, and has the curious distinction of being the first place I've seen where earlier in-migrants to Aspen, Santa Fe, Mendocino, etc. have moved to escape the tourist-trap mess those once pristine little communities have become. The pattern is relatively simple, and goes something like this:

Jack and Sally are fed up with life in suburban Marin County where increasing taxes, pollution, congestion, petty crime, major crime, adolescent dopers, post-adolescent dopers, spec home developers, stained glass, Victorian oak, interior shingles, old brick, chrome, leather, BMWs, and twenty-four-hour K-ROCK blasting the tympana of their functionally illiterate teenagers' ears finally drive them to hysteria. They've got to get out. Jack, a graphic artist who is able to set up a studio anywhere, looks around for a place to escape the dead-bolt insanity of his burglar-proofed life. Even his morning jog in nearby Mount Tamalpais Park has been curtailed by a lunatic called the Trailside Killer.

A friend tells Jack about Sandpoint. Quiet, cheap, incredibly beautiful. He goes to have a look and (as he tells Sally) is "blown away." The moment he can sell his house in Mill Valley he does so—for $350,000. He buys a four-bedroom, two-bath home on the Pend Oreille River a few miles from town—three fireplaces, recreation room with wet bar, wall-to-wall decks, and a hundred feet of river frontage with a dock—for $123,000. After capital gains he still socks away enough to live comfortably for the rest of his life on the interest alone, and this makes him so jubilant that when he returns to Mill Valley to collect his possessions he tells all his old friends about the nirvana he has stumbled into. He wants to let them in on it. They argue that "Sandpoke" sound pretty "out there" in the boondocks. Not so, Jack insists. Spokane is an hour away. Three hours' flight time from LAX. In fact a number of movie people, airline pilots, TV writers actually *commute* from Sandpoint.

The conclusion to this fiction is simple enough. Within two or three years Jack has recruited at least five of his old friends to the Sandpoint community, and several more are hedging their bets with "investment property" they plan soon to convert to a permanent residence.

Urban transplants change their habitat, but seldom their habits. It doesn't take very long before they begin to feel the need for services they took for granted in Marin County but that are not provided for in their new rural community—like a restaurant offering something more elegant than chicken-fried steak, a watering hole with a few ferns, etched glass, and strawberry daiquiris. Jack has never felt comfortable in that roustabout saloon with its overbearing jukebox and its endless Merle Haggard, Mel Tillis, Conway Twitty adenoidal yowling about big rigs and broken hearts. Come to think of it, an FM station with a mixture of classical and jazz might relieve the George Jones jitters he gets every time he turns on the car radio. And *somebody* ought to import something besides Almaden Chablis.

Somebody will, of course. Somebody will also open a chic boutique, a gallery, a coffeehouse, an art deco printshop, a foreign film cinema, a racquetball club, a jazzercise class, a summer crafts fair. Somebody has to gentrify the rednecks. Man does not live by Coors alone.

Most of the above amenities are already available in Sandpoint, though evidently in limited enough supply so as not to visibly compete—no billboard attempts to grab attention. One gets the feeling from wandering around the four-block square that constitutes downtown that real people still live here. Western Auto, State Farm, J. C. Penney, First Federal Savings, Sprouse-Reitz, White Dove Bookshoppe, Rexall, Self-Service TV. It lacks the fraudulent atmosphere of a Jackson Hole (to pick an extreme example) where counterfeit cowboys sprouting exotic chicken feathers from their Bailey straw hats have infused the business community with a hitching post mentality that turns everything authentically western into a parody of itself. In Sandpoint I see no wagon wheels, cigar-store Indians or elk-antler gazebos on the village green. Just an unpretentious town, neither run-down nor overdressed.

How long this will last seems uncertain. A "public

market" under construction on a bridge over Sand Creek in the heart of the downtown district is advertised as a future festival of "small shops, boutiques, food stands, and artisan booths." Sort of a Panhandle Ponte Vecchio, one might say, intended to define Sandpoint "as a center for tourism and the arts in the Northwest." It may never live up to its hopeful billing, but it strikes me as a clear sign of the direction in which the business community is trying to go.

Well, so what? An attractive lady who is one of the major forces behind a proposed Sandpoint music festival (and who is also in real estate) informs me that the region's economy can no longer depend on the declining timber industry, that tourism and recreational development are essential for survival. She says (in terms more elegant that I am able to remember) that those who are trying to promote Sandpoint are not attempting to run out the field-and-stream crowd, they are simply providing alternatives to tearing around in a lumbering, four-by-four gas hog with mag rims and meats (lug tires), blasting the declining game population to smithereens while Johnny "take this job and shove it" Paycheck comforts on the eight-track. What's wrong with attracting new people to the area, she asks rhetorically? What's wrong with gentrification?

Nothing. I guess. Especially if you work for one of the twenty-four real estate agencies in town. "But all this growth," I ask her timidly, "all these condos on the shore, second-home developments, fairs, festivals, ski weeks—don't they maybe reduce the quality of the quietude you came here for in the first place?"

"No."

Meaning that either she didn't come for that reason in

the first place, or they don't. I remember the woman I talked with in the library, and wonder if perhaps the native population would agree. At the very least it seems clear that it's not "hippies" who are changing the ambience of Sandpoint.

At the close of our interview my informant looks at me a moment and then says, "I certainly hope you're not going to write about the drug issue. We've had enough of that." Why is this such a touchy subject around here? Sandpoint's drug problems, by California standards, surely can't be worth mention—though the fact that I am continually warned away from it suggests it has caused some consternation among local residents. I *wasn't* going to write about it, but now I will.

III

As explained by a friend I meet for a drink at the Hydra, the "issue" amounts to a local resident having recently been busted in Miami with seven pounds of cocaine in her luggage, a teenage kid having killed a grocery clerk during a robbery to obtain money for a drug debt, and a few people arrested for growing marijuana. Sounds like a quiet, sedate town to me. But the most interesting consequence of all these events was an undercover investigation of drug trafficking secretly funded by seven outraged citizens—funded to the tune of $20,500. A narc-for-hire was brought in to set up "buys," the Federal Drug Enforcement Agency was supposed to provide the money, but when everything was ready to go the DEA claimed it had never heard of any such arrangement, the papers got wind of the whole business, and the great sting was blown out of the water. The narc fled town. Nobody got busted for anything.

An expensive lesson for the Sandpoint Seven. And the idea of private citizens funding law operations, though a cherished western tradition, may be more unnerving than how much whoopee weed is being smoked in the people's parlors on a Saturday night. Certainly a lot of local folks thought so, and expressed themselves on the subject of vigilantism to the Sheriff's Department, the City Council, and the local press. Old West vs. new West. The whole matter seems primarily to illustrate the conflicts of interest between traditional and new-age values that inevitably surface when a rural community begins to feel the pressure of an urban migration.

It is hard to imagine drug use of any kind in Sandpoint until rather recently. As I have said, newcomers change their habitat but seldom their habits. Our mythical Jack enjoyed his pharmaceuticals down in Mill Valley, and it doesn't occur to him to change his behavior just to conform to some backwoods mentality that equates dope with moral disintegration. Jack is no stone freak, no freebasing addict with an expensive habit. Why, he hardly toots a line a week—this week. But he represents a new market for a service not previously in demand. He introduces a foreign element—he and all the other young and restless, the Yuppie lawyers, artists, doctors, dentists, accountants, investors, business people whom the Chamber of Commerce is so eager to attract to the area. Its members should recognize (though they never do) that in-migrants bring with them attitudes and behavior that often run counter to the indigenous social patterns, and it should be no surprise to *anybody* that there are drugs in town. Their presence is indirectly courted.

The real question, however, is how Sandpoint will stand up to the more serious pressures for urbanization that its new population—all the while yearning for a simpler existence and marveling at the tranquility of rural life—inexorably brings to bear. The answer depends, of course, on the awareness (wariness?) of both old-timers and newcomers, and it is a crooked path beset by special interests who are often more interested in the aggrandizement of their bankroll than in the quality of their environment.

The old-timer may find that while the economic base of his town goes up as more and more of the affluent move in, his personal situation deteriorates. Not only little irritations like having to hunt for a parking place, wait in line at the market, suffer threats of zoning restrictions that will prohibit him from dividing his property between his children, learning to remember a six-digit telephone number instead of four, but an exponential increase in the cost of public services as the demand for new roads, sewers, power lines, and hookups becomes severe. Worst of all, the property taxes on his old homestead may rise to a point where he is unable, finally, to hold on to it any longer. He may get a good price for it from the developer when he sells; he may move to Sun City and take up killing snakes with a four-iron; but Sun City may not be quite what he had in mind for his golden years. More likely the old homestead will be whittled away to pay the taxes, and the golden years will be spent living with his daughter and her unamused husband. That, unfortunately, is a scenario that has been repeated in many places that were once like Sandpoint, Idaho.

And for the newcomers the dangers are quite simply

that by sheer force of numbers they begin to recreate the problems they moved to escape. Those problems, as any boomtown in the energy-rich West can testify, also increase exponentially. Not just pollution, congestion, and the proliferation of bureaucratic institutions. Suicides, wife beatings, aggravated assaults, child abuse, theft—all those unsavory little human activities—do not merely double as the population doubles, they increase by four to six times. It is an unhappy statistic. It leads people who have moved into the Garden of Eden to want to close the door and keep all others out. But isolationism is obviously as impossible as resisting all change. The only salvation for the rural in-migrant (it seems to me) is not only to consider whether he is going to live in the garden, but *how* he is going to live in it, how he is going to adapt and acculturate without disturbing its most salubrious features. (Naturally the first step is to pay strict attention to the uninvited preachings of transient writers who spend a few weeks filling up notebooks and then scram.)

As I drive back toward Spokane I go through that inevitable moment of journalistic misgiving. Who am I to carp, criticize, shake a warning finger at folks in a town I don't even live in? It's an old problem, and I come to my usual conclusion. Why not? I can't dance. I've seen enough places ruined by uncontrolled development, thoughtless living, ineffectual planning, to understand a bit of the process. I grew up in a place where the process, if not invented, was at least refined to the state of the art. Besides, Sandpoint is an idyllic place. Might like to move there myself. Host a summer writers' conference.

I guess not. I think I'm mainly motivated by the desire to go back in a few years and *not* find some variation on

Telluride or Jackson Hole. It seems to me enough remote enclaves of spectacular beauty have been trashed by those who make little attempt to understand their environment and those who are merely greedy for the second-home sale, the tourist buck. Unfortunately, in the long run, the only tourists and second-home owners who continue to visit these places are those who would never have noticed them in the first place.

10

Blowdown At Scotia

*T*HE RAIN STARTS WHEN WE cross the Mendocino/Humboldt County line. Light rain—a number 2 on the intermittent wiper control. The open, rolling hills of the wine country have long given way to the steeper, heavily forested mountains of the Eel River drainage, and the logging truck has replaced the tour bus as the major highway hazard, even when the visibility is good. By the time we reach Garberville the wipers are no longer intermittent; they're full speed ahead, and when at last we leave the road at the tiny town of Scotia and pull up to a cafe for something to eat, we can barely see to drive. I wonder out loud how our Earth First! buddies are enjoying eco-defense in this downpour, perched as they are on little platforms a couple hundred feet up in swaying redwood trees. Somewhere out there. "Political activists are impervious to weather and experience," Bud says. "Personally I'm into lunch first and earth later." He gets no argument from me. If my former student (and son of an old friend) is still in his aerie, the messages of concern for his health and safety that I've been asked to transport will keep a while longer. In fact, they'll probably keep forever since finding him would require an effort I'm little inclined to invest.

Scotia lies along the Eel River in a valley between the Kings Mountain Range and the Trinity National Forest. It is fifteen miles inland from Cape Mendocino, the most westerly point in the contiguous United States, and about twenty miles south of Humboldt Bay, the only seaport worth noticing between San Francisco and Coos Bay, Oregon. It is a place where the rain often falls. Honeydew, on the seaward side of the mountains, once reported 174 inches for the year—a record, to be sure, but not that far out of line. The leeward side of the Kings Range is more protected, but the difference, as today demonstrates, often seems marginal. The cafe windows are fogged on the inside from condensation, and the mill hands who stop for coffee on the way to their shifts leave an ever expanding puddle beneath the counter with their wet boots and streaming slickers. Outside the grey clouds snag in the Douglas fir that lines the ridge above the river, tattered hems drifting down the slopes to merge with the dank breath of Scotia's mill ponds.

Scotia is a company town owned board, shingle and nail by Pacific Lumber, the oldest and for 117 years the most environmentally responsible member of the local timber industry. It is community and workplace all in one—three hundred or so tidy little homes, a store, a coffee shop, a gas station, a laundry, a church, two huge sawmills; many of its inhabitants are second-, third-, even fourth-generation employees. It is an historical relic, an anachronism, one of the few remaining company towns in a West once full of company towns, and its days, for reasons both simple and complex, are sadly numbered. While it is not characteristic of me to mourn the passing of an environmentally destructive industry, or a part thereof, I live in a wooden house (glass too), acknowledge that the world needs wood products, and understand that there will be companies to provide them. Pacific lumber was among the best. In Scotia it was generally understood that a respectable way of life depended on husbandry of the resources that sustained it.

Scotia's days are numbered for reasons that few people perched on the stools in this cafe could have imagined ten years ago. Or five years ago. Back then few of these folks had ever heard of insider trading, arbitrage, hostile takeovers, the corporate raider, Ivan Boesky, Carl Icahn, T. Boone Pickens, Drexel Burnham, or any of the other buzz names and buzzwords that became synonymous with the world of speculative finance during the reign of the man Herb Caen has dubbed King Ronald the Popular. Certainly none of them had ever heard of Charles Hurwitz or Maxxam Group Inc. The name Charles Hurwitz did not loom large in the lexicon of lumber in the early 1980s. Georgia Pacific, Louisiana Pacific, Simpson, Arco, Doug fir, piss fir, old growth, second growth, clear-cut, sustained yield, THPs—maybe even *EPIC vs. Johnson,* the Z'berg-Nejedly Act, or Gerald L. Partain, director of the California Department of Forestry. But Charles Hurwitz? From Texas? Home of the cow and the country singer? No one in the red heart of the redwood empire had ever heard of him.

Until, that is, one fall in 1985 when the telephone rang at 5:30 in the morning at the San Francisco home of Gene Elam, president and chief executive officer of the Pacific

Lumber Company. The voice at the other end, the voice of the aforementioned Houston financier (and chief executive officer of something called Maxxam) informed a groggy Mr. Elam that when the markets opened on the East Coast he was going to make an offer of $746 million for Pacific Lumber: $36 a share, $7 a share more than its current listing on the New York Stock Exchange. Unless, of course, Mr. Elam was in a mood for a *friendly* merger. He had about thirty minutes to think about it. Mr. Elam was reportedly noncommittal, though he was shortly in consultation with Pacific Lumber's attorneys, the distinguished firm of Wachtell, Lipton, Rosen and Katz, and thereafter the mood was not anything that could be described as friendly. The mood was to resist.

Pacific Lumber was unusual in the timber business not simply because a sense of security—longevity (almost tenure)—went with a job in its woods and mills, or because it inspired a "family" feeling among its employees, or because it paid $8000 a year toward the college tuition of workers' children, or because it maintained a town with cheap rent and all the conveniences. It was unusual because it conducted its operation as if it intended to go on operating well into the twenty-first century. It maintained a harvesting policy based on the inspired conviction that timber is a renewable resource, that selective logging, not clear-cutting, is the way to sustain yield, that carefully measuring profit rather than maximizing profit is the way to insure a protracted corporate life. Pacific Lumber counted its worth in something other than board feet, and the fact that in 1985 it remained one of a handful of timber companies still in business, healthily in business, in a county that once boasted more than three hundred sawmills was empirical evidence that its policies were sound. It paid good dividends to its stockholders, was debt free, maintained a loyal work force, had enough old-growth redwood to cut for forty years and enough second growth to cut in perpetuity, was the darling of environmentalists. Just the kind of corporation one might like to raid.

The purely pragmatic mind might measure P-L's worth in less ideological terms. Pacific Lumber owned 193,000 acres of trees, including about forty percent of the remaining old-growth redwood outside of parks that could still be harvested, a $200-million welding and cutting division called Victor Equipment, corporate headquarters in San Francisco worth $32 million, 2,500 acres of timberlands south of San Francisco in San Mateo County, and a $50-million surplus in its company pension plan. Estimates of the overall value varied, but it was thought that the acreage alone would bring between $1.2 and $2 billion.

Not surprising, then, that the pragmatic Hurwitz and associates were willing to offer $746 million for P-L, or that they were willing to counter the resistance put up by Mr. Elam and his board of directors by increasing that offer from $36 a share to $38.50, and finally to $40. Pacific Lumber management refused the first of these offers, filling a suit along the way that charged Hurwitz with violations of securities laws and calling him "a notorious takeover artist" whose history of dealings demonstrated "a conspicuous absence of integrity, competence and fitness necessary to control or manage a substantial business enterprise." (No mention in the suit, because not then known, of the substantial amount of P-L stock acquired by Ivan Boesky three days before Hurwitz made his offer public, a purchase still under investigation by the securities and commodities fraud unit in the Manhattan U.S. Attorney's Office.) But in the end it was difficult, if not impossible, to reject an offer of $40 a share for a stock listed at $29. Pacific Lumber management risked lawsuits from their own institutional investors if they failed to maximize value, and so, on October 22 the "merger" went through. Pacific Lumber became the ward of a company of real estate speculators from the East Coast— which is even farther from the red heart of the redwood empire than Texas. One employee summed up the sentiment of many toward this buy-out. "I lost a part of me," he said, "but there's nothing you can do. This is just a job now."

II

The rain abates for a while and Bud and I walk down along the river. Logging trucks up on the highway contest with the whine of saws in Mill A (or is it B?), chewing through an endless parade of former trees that are being fed by a giant conveyor from the debarker into the mouth of the building. Conversation is limited. On the other hand, conversation with Bud is always limited. "Thimbleberry," he says, pointing to a bank of vegetation. "Oregon grape." We pause before a stadium-size parking lot filled with stacks of new lumber. "Ecocide waits for no man," he says.

From the look of things it doesn't seem to have made much difference that Pacific Lumber was gobbled up by the Maxxam Group Inc., which in turn was eaten by (merged with) yet another Charles Hurwitz enterprise, MCO Holdings Inc. (Cynics have suggested that this move was to help obfuscate illegal activities associated with the initial buy-out.) The mills are humming; the trucks are running. People are working ten-hour shifts, six days a week, drawing overtime. The company hired a number of new workers and bought another sawmill in an adjacent town to handle the overload. But there have been changes that have nothing to do with growth and prosperity, changes that are less visible but that lead people to question how long all this will last. It's "just a job now"; don't make any long-range plans.

For one thing, in spite of financier Hurwitz's assurances at the time of the buy-out that Maxxam Group was "a builder, not a liquidator," many of the new management's first acts were clearly preparatory to liquidation. Maxxam incurred a huge debt when it paid nearly $900 million for P-L. And when MCO bought up Maxxam within a year and a half, financing much of that merger with $575 million in junk bonds, it still had a reported debt of $550 million, with interest-only payments of $39.4 million a year. Which is $5.4 million more than P-L *made* in 1985. P-L cut 137 million board feet of lumber for an earnings of $34 million. What to do about this discrepancy? It doesn't take a first-year student in economics to figure it out.

After buying Maxxam, MCO begin dismantling its acquisition. It sold the corporate headquarters in San Francisco for $32 million. It put Victor Equipment on the block. It put its 2,500 acres of San Mateo County up for sale. And it bought an insurance annuity to guarantee the assets in the P-L pension plan, then withdrew $35 million in cash from that plan and applied it to the debt. Worst of all, it proposed to double the annual acreage to be logged, from the old pace of 137 million board feet to

270 million, and it started clear-cutting old-growth red-wood as fast as it could. It threw out, one might say, a 117-year policy of selective cutting, threw out the entire concept of sustained yield (mandated, incidentally, by the 1973 California Forest Practice Act), threw out the very concept on which Pacific Lumber was founded in the first place.

No doubt increasing the cut in order to increase profits seemed logical to the pragmatic mind, particularly the pragmatic mind that knows little about the lumber business. But the price of redwood, as people in the lumber business *do* know, is in part a function of its scarcity. Doubling its availability in the market drives the value down, not up—which is precisely what happened in Humboldt. The stumpage price for second-growth redwood fell five percent in one year. And of course doubling the cut of a finite resource like virgin redwood reduces by one-half the number of years one is going to be in the virgin redwood business. What the new Pacific Lumber did, in short, was reduce the value of its most abundant product, second growth, and accelerate the demise of its most precious product, old growth. It concocted arguments to prove that facts weren't facts, but to a number of observers the new policies seemed to have everything to do with liquidation and nothing to do with building. They sounded, indeed, a lot like "cut and run."

If doubling the harvest was debatable as an economic move, in all other respects it was stupid. Morally stupid. Intellectually stupid. Politically stupid. Nobody outside a company cares much about the sale of a corporate headquarters, or a cutting and welding subsidiary, or even 2,500 acres of San Mateo County. Nobody much cares about a disenfranchised Pacific Lumber "family" except members of that family. Nobody is terribly concerned about the fate of a "company town" like Scotia except the people who live in it. But start cutting the last of the virgin redwoods, start threatening old-growth dependent species like the marbled murrelet, the red mountain vole, the spotted owl, start messing up a watershed with your clear-cuts, your skidders, loaders, and haulers, and you have executed a spectacular belly flop in the eecow pie. Because now you have attracted the attention of a broad coalition of those people you basically hold in contempt, those people who care deeply about the natural environment and who are prepared to try anything, from taking you to court to roosting in the tops of your trees to stop you. They may even drive a few hundred spikes into your future saw logs. You have also attracted the attention of environmentally sensitive state and local politicians, like, say, northern California's Senator Barry Keene. Senator Keene will observe that "California can't afford to allow the financing of corporate takeovers through the liquidation of our redwood and fir forests," and will promptly introduce legislation to establish fixed limits on forest degradation. All of the above is precisely what happened when Pacific Lumber decided to double its timber harvest in Humboldt County.

III

We debate the likelihood of actually finding my former student in the vast expanse of Six Rivers National Forest, and Bud, who is unclear why we are not by now fly-fishing in the Marble Mountain Wilderness as planned, asks what is supposed to happen if we do locate him up there on Salmon Creek, Owl Creek, Booth's Run Creek, Shaw Creek, Yager Creek, Chadd Creek, Stitz Creek, or any of the other endlessly possible creeks. What do we say? "Hey Rufus, your dad says hi? He says he admires your courage and supports your principles. Your mom says come down outta there this minute."

"I was hoping if we found him we could persuade a logger to cut his tree out from under him and I could make some money writing an angry denunciation of state-supported terrorism in the wilderness. Rufus *in memoriam*."

"What has the state got to do with this?" Bud says, although he knows very well. "Let's go fishing."

Indeed, what Rufus and his Earth First! *compadres* are campaigning against with their tree-in is not only the destruction of old-growth forests, but the collusion in this process between the timber industry and the California Department of Forestry. The CDF, among other things, is supposed to review timber harvest plans and enforce the regulations mandated by the California Forest Practice Act and the California Environmental Quality Act (CEQA). It is supposed to disapprove those plans that do not meet the standards established by law. But for their performance in this role, alas, we must assign them a grade of F and put them on academic probation. How they got into this school in the first place is a mystery.

In 1985 the State Appellate Court ruled in *EPIC vs. Johnson* that the CEQA is an integral part of the regulations governing logging, and that both timber companies and the CDF must consider all significant adverse cumulative environmental effects that a timber harvest plan may have on a given area. A significant environmental effect, says the CEQA, "means a substantial, or *potentially substantial* [italics mine] adverse change in any of the physical conditions within the area affected by the project including land, air, water, minerals, flora, fauna, ambient noise and objects of historic or aesthetic significance." Reasonable people might argue over how much adverse change constitutes "substantial" or "potentially substantial" change, but observe how the CDF addresses the problem. The following is representative, quoted from the Pre-harvest Inspection Report for the South Fork of Yager Creek:

> Tractor logging and new road construction will contribute to surface soil erosion, but it is unlikely to be significant at this time . . .

> Mass soil movement may happen . . . but to say that it will be significant is to [sic] early . . .

> New road construction and tractor logging may somewhat decrease water quality, but only for a short time period. It cannot be judged at this time if it will be significant . . .

> This stand of old-growth timber has direct access to the public, however, it cannot be judged at this time if aesthetics would be significantly impacted . . .

> No endangered species were noted during the inspection. Old-growth timber has been noted to shelter all types of plants and animals. Unless one

observes these species it cannot be judged if any significant impact would occur.

Graded on the basis of grammar, syntax, and spelling alone this essay does not represent passing work. The most endangered species is the English language. Judged for its content it demonstrates a distinct lack of effort on the part of its author, or authors. It is not doublethink, it is no-think at all. It is evasion, pure and simple. The California Department of Forestry has no idea, it claims, whether the proposed logging has even a *potential* for causing significant erosion, or a decrease in water quality, or an impact on the scenery. It acknowledges that old-growth timber is said to provide habitat for a variety of endangered species, but since it didn't see any (it doesn't say how hard it looked) it can't say "at this time" whether any will be affected. At what time, one wonders, *will* it be able to answer the required questions?

It is possible, of course, that the CDF is, in fact, as incompetent as its inspection reports suggest, that it has no powers of observation, no memory, no imagination, no capacity to project what *potential* effect denuding 125 acres of virgin timber along Yager Creek might have, that it has never seen a 17-ton tractor at work or listened to a battery of chain saws, that it is unable to make an aesthetic distinction between a moonscape and a cathedral of two-thousand-year-old redwoods. But at this time, I doubt it. At this time I'm inclined to believe that the only significant impact that concerns it is the impact on the pocketbook of its patron, Big Timber. The CDF approved timber harvest plans in 1987 for the four biggest wood-products companies (Simpson, Georgia Pacific, Louisiana Pacific, and Pacific Lumber) that amounted to approximately 109,295 acres in northwestern California alone. Their denial rate is less than one percent per annum. Why wouldn't it be? By their own admission they don't seem to know what effect a project is going to have until after it has taken place.

IV

The steam whistles on Scotia's mills have started to blow, signifying . . . we know not what. Perhaps it is already noon. Or the end of a shift. Or 5:00. Bud has initiated his own protest by removing his fly rod from the back of the truck and practicing his cast in the parking lot. I get the idea. He's trying to tell me we are accomplishing no useful purpose here and we are catching no fish. Still, I can't help pointing out to my yawning companion that it's an interesting demographic sub-study, this. The destruction of the natural environment we take for granted. We know they're going to take those trees down one way or another today or tomorrow. They never quit. But seldom does one have such an immediate and obvious paradigm of the consequences of environmental indifference to the human habitat. Almost at once a social indifference sets in. The continuity of dependence on a natural resource is broken, and the community begins to unravel. "Over the years there was an obligation to the community," said one employee who had been in Scotia for thirty-two years, "and with the change in ownership that obligation will be lessened." It will be lessened, he might have added, because of a change in attitude reflected by that ownership— attitude toward people, attitude toward product. "If you take care of the resources and take care of the people and put out a good product," said Warren Murphy, grandson of A. Stanwood Murphy (who ran the company until 1961) and son of Stanwood A. Murphy (who ran it until 1972), "everything else runs itself. What will be missing now is that whole paternal feeling."

What will also be missing is the sense of history that goes with that paternalism, and the sense of being a *part* of that history. As the man said, it's just a job now. Or in the words of another, "an era has ended with this merger. People aren't going to feel that this is home the way they did, or that they can put down roots here." Indeed, people are pulling up the roots they had put down, some of them rather deeply. Gene Elam is gone. Warren Murphy quit and moved out of Scotia. A number of workers who feared rent increases (correctly) sold their stock in the company to buy their own homes in other communities. The accelerated depletion of the natural resource has its parallel depletion in the human resource. Noting the historical inseparability of Scotia's community and workplace, its pastor, Steve Frank, remarked, "After the takeover, people saw that way of life as being vulnerable. And the question is, will that way of life be maintained over time?"

I think not. Even if Earth First! saves some of the old growth. Even if the courts insist that the California Forest Practice Act and the CEQA regulations be adhered to. Even if Senator Barry Keene's legislation is passed. I think not. Charles Hurwitz was too big a hurricane, and he blew down Scotia.

11

Living off the Fat of the Land

*I*T HAS BEEN SAID THAT the phrase "The Great State of California" refers less to a place between the Sierra Nevada and the Pacific Ocean than to an illusion—a dream dump or lotus land fantasy, depending on the mood of your day—and that all attempts to unify it in social, cultural, even geographic terms seem doomed to frustration because none of it is quite like anywhere else and all of it is sort of like somewhere else and most of it is just passing by anyway, here today, replaced tomorrow. Perhaps we should rename it "The Great State of Mind."

I think John Steinbeck defined it best when he outlined his microcosm in Monterey, Cannery Row, and he could have been writing about a thousand locations in California when he told us Cannery Row was "a poem, a stink, a grating noise, a quality of light, a tone, a habit, a nostalgia, a dream." Cannery Row is right across the bay from Santa Cruz, the poem and stink I came to live in twenty-five years ago, and like Santa Cruz it has not been much improved by time and the tides of tourism, transients, and testosterone. At least in my view. I recently described my home town in a book called *American Places* as the ultimate laid-back, tripped-out joss house of cognitive centering, the last mecca of mellow, the environment one seeks when one is in the mood for a cosmic tuneup. Or a lid. Or a gram of nose candy. I was not voted citizen of the year for my opinions.

It was a grumpy and hostile evaluation, no doubt, and I meant every word of it. But even as I enjoyed the howls of anguish that went up from local boosters, snickered at the florid rebuttals in the local paper by members of the city council, I was forced by the hullabaloo to acknowledge that my true self—the kind, cheerful, generous, reverent, fun-loving neighbor that I really am—had been overshadowed once again by the snarling voice of my alter ego, Fang the Curmudgeon.

Therefore . . . the three episodes that follow are an atonement, my tribute to those earlier days (not so long ago at that) when it was still possible to entertain the illusion of rugged independence out here in the land of the setting sun. My nostalgia and dream, my tone and quality of light. While I admit that they employ a few devices of fiction, they are essentially the truth. None of the names have been changed to protect the guileless, chuckleheaded innocents who participated in the search for a free lunch in Eden (down, Fang), and none of the details have been embellished—much. They contain no environmentalist angst, no finger-wagging warnings of ecological disaster, no condemnation of the federal stewards employed to assist in the multiple abuse of our public lands. These little paradigms seem, as such, a fitting conclusion to an otherwise cheerless appraisal of man's relationship with his surroundings.

Heading for the Last Roundup

One evening not long after my former wife and I had returned to the United States from a three-year stint in the Peace Corps in Ecuador, we were having dinner with some old friends who live in the mountains behind Santa Cruz. My wife was describing the petrifying experience of walking into an American supermarket for the first time in three years, marvelling at the incredible number of choices offered on every shelf, even as she lamented our inability to buy any of them. It was major culture shock not being able to make up one's mind about all of the things one couldn't afford anyway.

For my part, I was lamenting a number of changes in the ambience that I have associated with Santa Cruz, California, since I first began to frequent its beaches back in the early 1950s. It has always been a place for me where simple pleasures and inexpensive living were available to anyone who wanted them. A few short years ago the downtown was a nice, funky, run-down collection of crummy shops owned by Portuguese and Italians who had been around forever. Now it is gussied up with a mall, and redwood benches that are too low for old people to sit on, and a mini Ghirardelli Square where you can buy embroidered blouses from Guatemala or French cookware or creative playthings of one kind and another, and where you can walk around in a funny hat with all the other freaks in funny hats and hope that someone notices.

"They moved the United Cigar Store," I said to Eamon Barrett, my host. "They're messing with our institutions. What happened to the Fun Club? What became of living off the land? Where has all the style gone?"

Eamon shrugged. At this moment his wife produced from the oven a roast beef so large and succulent that I began to fidget. Meat was certainly one of the institutions that had died during my time in South America. Everybody I knew had become a tofu addict, a whining vegetarian, a sprout-eating geek, sipping herbal teas while contemplating the colon. "Have no illusions about my affluence," Eamon warned me as we sat down to his roast, "and if you brought your buck knife, I think I'd get it out. This protein is homegrown and apt to be a mite tough."

"You grew it?" I said.

"We live off the fat of the land," he said.

"You're serious? You raised a steer?"

"You too can raise a steer." Eamon has a habit of looking sly when he talks, no matter what he is saying. You never know when he is putting you on.

"You just tell me how, man," I said. "And quickly. Spare me the details."

"Well, what you do," he replied, sawing at his meat, "is you go to the auction in Salinas on a Saturday, buy yourself a calf for around forty or fifty bucks, bring him back and put him in my pasture until he weighs about a thousand pounds, and you eat him."

"How much land do you need for this enterprise?" I asked.

"Four or five acres."

"How much land do you have?"

"About forty acres."

My wife evidently perceived what was coming. "It would take us two years to go through a whole cow," she said. "It would spoil long before we could use it."

"I'll go halves with you," Eamon said. "Or you get a couple of guys and we'll buy two calves and split up the work four ways."

"Work?"

"A little fence mending."

"Fantastic," I said. "The cattle business. Saddle tramps and riding the range and all that. Singing songs around the campfire with one's sidekicks. Living on the land. Now that's bringing back style, all right."

"There's nothing to it," Eamon said.

And that is how it all began. I told Jim Houston and Jim told Forrest Robinson. We had a little meeting, drank a little whiskey, and formed the *As Is Cattlemen's Association of Santa Cruz County.* Two middle-aged writers, a professor of American literature, and a mick mathematician with forty acres in his backyard. We were not completely out of control. We set ourselves a limit of thirty bucks apiece, or sixty for a cow. "That's my top dollar," Houston said. "How much do you think we can do for sixty dollars, Eamon?"

"We'll go Saturday and see," Eamon said. "But for sixty bucks we can buy a herd."

Eamon's truck is a disgraceful old wreck. The horn doesn't work and the taillights are out. So are the brakes. It's mostly rust and wire, and one fender flaps like a broken wing, but fortunately the fog is so thick all the way from the coast to the Salinas Valley that we don't have to worry about the highway patrol. A good thing too.

Once I got a speeding ticket on the way home from gathering mussels up near Davenport, and the fine ran the price of dinner that night to about five bucks a swallow. You can't live very well off the land, or the sea, that way.

About nine o'clock we pull into the auction grounds and coast to a stop, peer through the mist at the parking lot and the holding pens, both empty and without a sign of life, peer at Eamon, our resident expert, peer at each other. Eamon climbs out of the pickup and shrugs. "Maybe the auction's on Sundays," he says.

"We thought you'd been here before," we say.

"I was."

"On what *day* were you here before?"

"I think it was Saturday." He looks around slyly. "Hey, I remember a kind of coffee shop around the side of that barn. I think. Maybe we can get something to eat."

There is, in fact, a coffee shop. And there is, in fact, an auction, only it starts at noon. Eamon reminds us that he did not specify a time, and that, in any case, a self-respecting ranch hand gets up at the crack of dawn regardless. So we should be pleased with ourselves and kindly climb the hell off his back. As there is no alternative, we settle down to a glazed doughnut and a cup of coffee.

Cattle trucks start to roll in and unload sometime around ten, and the four of us mosey over to the pens where a crowd of authentic-looking farmers have gathered to look over today's bill of fare. You have to see this to believe it. Here we are all dressed up in our cowboy hats and boots, talking out of the sides of our mouths and standing around with our thumbs hooked in our Levi's pockets, and our thighs sort of thrust forward and out, like we're not too familiar with *walking* I mean, we *look* pretty good. In fact I look a lot like Clint Eastwood, only better. We look as if we do this kind of thing all the time—buying cows, selling cows; we're cattlemen, right? and we're just out here hanging around the chutes swapping lies before the big action starts inside and we get down to the squint-eyed business of serious dealing. Houston makes a passable Lee Van Cleef. Eamon looks like a sod-busting Eli Wallach, but he'll do. Robinson . . . well, Robinson has on these *tennis* shoes. *White* tennis shoes, with little faggy blue stripes down the side. The rest of us keep sidling away.

We're feeling a bit foolish anyway, standing there in our Charlie Tweedle Stetsons and our $24.95 Acme boots with the stitching on the toes and the red, white, and blue plastic eagle inlaid up the side. We don't know one cow from another, and by now it is clear that Eamon doesn't either. Sure, he's done this before and lived, but obviously by a streak of dumb luck. I hear a lot of talk going on around us about drop calves, weaners, Holsteins, Herefords, and heifers, Angus and white-face, Angus cross. One fellow points to a group of four calves and says, "Them's gonna make it." His companion nods emphatically and spits a stream of tobacco juice in the direction of another group nearby. "Them ain't." I look from one bunch to the other about fifteen times, but for the life of me I can't see the slightest difference.

After a while I give up on the calves and sneak over by a chute where some large, very fat steers are being unloaded and prodded down an alley into pens. A cowboy standing next to me watches them go by, shakes his head, and says, more or less in my direction, "Sheeitsake, will you looka' that." For a moment I think he's referring to me, but no, it's something so obvious that no reply is expected. He hooks a toe between the rails of the fence and contemplates the disgraceful arrivals. "Must of kept 'em dry a week' fore they let 'em at a trough," he says.

"Must of," I say.

"Poor ass-hoe buys them's gonna get some purty soggy beef."

"For a fact," I tell him. I haven't the slightest idea what this conversation is all about, but I keep my cover intact. Right now I'm just worried about how to tell a Holstein from a Hereford-Angus cross, since they're both black and white, have four legs and a tail, and go moo.

"What difference does it make?" Robinson asks.

"One is for eating and one is for milking," I tell him. I know that much, at least. I'm not wearing tennis shoes.

Robinson chews the skin on his lip for a while as he thinks this over. "Ah ha. I see. Different cow, different function. This adds complexity."

Eamon, who has been wandering around inside the auction barn and apparently asking *questions,* comes trotting over with a look of confidence on his face and informs us that things are once again under control. "Here's the deal," he says. "What we're after is an Angus or a Hereford or an Angus-Hereford cross. A bull calf. Don't go bidding on heifers. Now we don't want anything under three hundred pounds because that way we're pretty sure that whatever we buy isn't going to up and die on us, and we want to hang back on the bidding because all the amateurs get a wild hair the first eight or ten calves that come out, and after that things simmer down a bit. There's nothing to it."

"Oh yeah? Well tell us this, Mr. County Extension Agent, these bulls and heifer . . . how do you tell them apart?" The poser of this question requests anonymity.

Charter members of the As Is Cattlemen's Association are convulsed. *"Haw haw haw, har har harrrrr.* You simple ass, one has tits and one has testes."

"Is that so? The reason I ask is that I'm standing here looking over about two dozen calves, and as far as I can see none of them has *either* of the items you mention."

Pause. Silence. There seems some truth . . .

Auction time is getting closer, and unless we are willing to go home skunked, we're going to have to get some answers fast. Eamon Barrett's ten-year-old son, Aaron, whom I haven't mentioned before because I didn't think he'd come in handy, suddenly strikes my imagination as a possible solution to a lot of problems. There is nothing shameful about a small boy asking questions of his elders, especially if we move off to the side and explain that he doesn't belong with us. No sir, he's none of our business, the dumb kid, running around asking people how you tell the ladies from the gents. "You see this quarter, Aaron," I say, "and you see that guy over there that looks like Marshal Dillon? I want you to go ask him . . ."

Aaron agrees, and trots off. Robinson and I light up a Marlboro.

In less than five minutes he is back. "Holstein heifers are going around fifty-eight to sixty-five; bulls around fifty-two. Guernseys about the same. Hereford and Angus bulls from fifty-eight to sixty-eight, if they're under four hundred pounds. Heifers less. Drop calves by the head and ranging from thirty-seven to forty-five depending on . . ."

"Hold it, Aaron, hold it. You're not the morning farm report. Thirty-seven to forty-five what? What are we talking about here? Dollars? Cents per pound? Gestation period?"

"How should I know?" Aaron says. "I'm just telling you what the guy told me."

"Never mind. Did you find out how to tell the males from the females?"

Aaron snorts. "When were *you* guys born?"

In the auction arena we take seats and sit quietly while the bidding begins on the goats. They are paraded out one by one and whipped into a frenzied little dance by the auctioneer's assistants in the ring, two adolescent morons in undersized hats and oversized zits who chew gum, smoke, and look bored. The effort is obviously a strain. They have to be repeatedly reminded by their puppeteer to get the animals out of the ring once they have been sold. It seems like a lot to remember.

Sometime between the sale of pigs and horse-meat, Jim leans over and regards me with the mariner's eye. "There has been a new dimension added to this caper," he says. "I've been doing a little figuring and a four-hundred-pound calf times sixty cents a pound, assuming we can get one for that, comes to $240. Two hundred and forty dollars is somewhat in excess of our top figure ... $180 in excess, the way I add it up, and so I'm beginning to wonder about this whole deal. It's not exactly the giveaway you advertised."

Penny-pinching is what one expects from Jim. "Hang in there," I whisper. "Let's see if we can get one at around two hundred pounds. That ought to be safe enough, and it would only be sixty bucks apiece."

"Twice what we agreed to," Jim mutters, but he ruminates on it for a few minutes. "Okay, but sixty is my absolute limit."

In addition to the previously mentioned information that we do not have about the cattle business, add the following. We have absolutely no conception of the size or age of a two-hundred-pound cow. When the goats and pigs and sheep have all been sold, when we finally get down to the main event, beef on the hoof, we discover to our horror that the *smallest* calf, still wobbling on its pins and wet from—birth?—weighs in at around 150.

"We've got a problem," Jim murmurs in my ear.

"Yet another dimension," I observe sourly. "If we're going to get anything old enough to be sure of its survival, we're going to have to go higher. What do you think?"

"Oh man, I dunno. Maybe two-fifty?"

"It's only another fifteen bucks a piece."

We sit and watch while the drop calves are auctioned off, calculating in our heads, trying to remember the last figure in the checkbook, anticipating the howl that is going to go up at home when the truth comes out. Just about this time a fine-looking Hereford calf trots in, weighing about 270 pounds (weights are flashed on a scale behind the auctioneer), and Eamon says "Hot damn, that sucker's mine." The bidding starts low and climbs grudgingly to around fifty-one cents a pound.

"Pretty cheap," I remark offhandedly to the guy on my right.

He flicks me a glance and says something that I translate as "Noah's snot."

"I beg your pardon?"

"S'not cheap for a *heifer*."

Eamon's bid of fifty-two has just been topped by a half when I lean over and jab him in the ribs. "Heifer," I croak.

"Say what?"

"A milk cow. A lady. No nads."

Eamon's salvation, however, is briefly enjoyed. A few minutes later, thinking he is buying an Angus steer, he outbids the field on a Holstein bull, and comes in a winner at ten cents a pound higher than the going rate. But we don't find this out until after the auction. For the moment he is one happy cowperson.

Houston and I are cleverly hanging back, waiting for the right breed, gender, and weight. After about half an hour a good-looking animal comes out, strong and sleek, a healthy Black Angus with filet mignon written all over him, and the auctioneer starts in his mile-a-minute patter. *FiftyfivefivefivefivefivefiveFIVEwho'llgimmeesixsixsixsixSIX I got six who'll make it sevensevenseven . . .*

I take a fast glance at the scale markings before they disappear, and am amazed to see that only 275 pounds is registered. A little more than we agreed on during our fifth recalculation, but such a gorgeous piece of meat, and he seems a lot bigger . . . Jim and I nod to each other, and up goes my finger. Fifty-seven. Somebody makes it fifty-eight. I go fifty-nine. The opposition says sixty, and at this point I begin to get cold feet. Pausing to think, I put my finger in my nose . . . and learn the symbol for a half-cent raise. Sixty and a half is enough, it turns out, to buy us a cow.

Shaking hands, we pick up our tag and head up the alley where you pay your money and get a pink slip that lets you take your prize home. It's a little more than we'd agreed on, but what the hell. We're jubilant. We did it. We bought a freezer full of beef. I feel like Ernest Hemingway in that picture where he's standing with his fishing pole and his shit-eating grin and a twelve-foot marlin hanging from the dockside hoist. But then I notice that

Jim, who has taken the slip from the lady behind the counter, has gone a little pale and is looking vaguely around himself like a dog about to lie down. His hat has slid so that it's bending out the tips of his ears, and his eyes have the worried look of a twelfth-round contender. He's developed a list to starboard. "What's the matter with you?" I say. He hands me the bill. It appears I read the scales wrong. Our cow weighs *four* hundred and seventy-five pounds. That'll be cash on the barrel head, son. $287.38.

We are no longer speaking. We slog out to the pickup, help push it around the parking lot until it starts, and follow it down to the loading chute. It's raining, of course, and my $29 Charlie Tweedle is beginning to melt. Gone are the chuck wagon witticisms, the *esprit de corps,* the "atta pepper" enthusiasm with which we began this miserable venture. Gone is my bank account. The kid who helps load the animals brings Eamon's Holstein, and it goes quietly enough into the truck. Our behemoth, however, wants no part of that broken-down Chebby. He is finally persuaded by an electric cattle prod to give it a try, but once he discovers he's trapped he begins to bust everything in sight. He butts the rear window and cracks it, kicks a piece out of the side rail, jams his leg through a rotten floor-board, and falls down. "You want to watch that sumbitch," the kid says.

"So what are we going to call him?" Robinson asks brightly.

Houston looks at him in disbelief.

"Humbert Humbert," I say. "Thus far he's screwed us girls everyway but loose."

"I'd tie his head low," the kid says. "So he can't climb out."

"Eamon is going to call the Holstein 'As Is'," Robinson says.

"When you get him castrated," the kid says, "he'll calm down."

"Robinson?" Houston asks.

The conclusions to be drawn from our day at the auction are so obvious that they hardly need examination. But the fact is we could have done much worse than Humbert Humbert and As Is, and if we paid a few cents more a pound than we should have, or made ourselves look a little silly, no serious damage done. Come to think of it, we had fun. And we will each wind up with nearly three hundred pounds of meat for which we will have paid about $150. That comes to around fifty cents a pound. Not bad. Nothing to it.

Except . . . ah, there are a few *hidden* expenses that should be itemized. On the return trip to Santa Cruz Eamon decides he'll ride in the back of the truck with the cattle, just in case Humbert decides to commit suicide on the interstate and deprive us of the pleasure of nipping his buds. So to speak. Castration is mild in comparison to the fantasies that lurk in the depths of our collective consciousness. We are traveling at thirty miles an hour along a ten-mile stretch of two-lane road that leads to the freeway, and although Robinson, who is driving, is unaware of it (there being no rearview mirror) about two hundred cars are stacked up behind us, and they are definitely being . . . *impeded*. That's the word the highway patrolman uses when he pulls us over to the side and starts writing out the ticket. "Impeding traffic," he says, and launches into a boring recitation on the perils of poking. "You guys got cars stuck behind you all the way back to Monterey."

"Is that a fact," Robinson says.

"Yeah. And I'm the guy who picks up the pieces after people like you . . ." The cop stops in mid-sentence and begins to look at Eamon's Chevy. "By the way, what is this . . . vehicle?"

"Cattle truck," Robinson says.

"Okay, wise guy, why don't we try the lights on this cattle truck and just make sure they work." Robinson pulls the switch. "Try the dimmers." Robinson hits the dimmers, and the cop pulls out his ticket book. "Horn?" Broken. "Side mirrors?" No glass. "Brake lights?" Out.

The inspection proves too much for Humbert, and he decides to climb up in the cab with the rest of us. There is a shower of glass as his head goes through the rear window, a wet muzzle smacks me in the ear, and there is a general competition to see who can bellow the loudest.

"Your vehicle has no back window," the patrolman says.

When he has finished writing all this up and gone off down the road in his four-hundred-horsepower economy special, and we're left sitting in the wreckage, we total up the citations and figure out that the price of beef has just gone up twenty-five cents a pound.

In the cattle business it's the hidden expenses that kill you. You get nickeled and dimed to death. A bale of alfalfa here, a salt lick there, a roll of barbed wire to mend the fence where your cows tore it up, bandages to mend the skin where the barbed wire tore *it* up, sacks of corn at $8.50 a hundredweight. You discover that in order to get good meat you have to grain your animals, at least during the last three hundred pounds of gain. You discover that it take eight pounds of grain to a pound of gain, and if you're paying eight cents a pound for the *grain,* you can just add sixty-four cents to the final per-pound cost of your *hamburger.* And then, of course, you have your medical expenses. These can vary tremendously, depending on the health and vigor of your cows and cowboys. Let me explain.

On the Saturday after the auction, early in the morning, we meet at the As Is Cattle Ranch for what our jester, Forrest Robinson, keeps referring to as "the roundup." Time has mellowed us. We are not in a rage with Humbert Humbert; we just hate him with a dull frontal ache, and we are mildly hysterical at the prospect of his mutilation.

"Eamon, how big is that pasture?"

Eamon informs us again that it is forty acres. "Our strategy is to drive the herd down into one corner; then all we do is lay a rope over them."

"Have you ever done this before?"

"All the time."

"Man, I'm telling you," Robinson says, "if five men and two boys can't catch one lousy calf before it's time for the champagne brunch, then we ought to hang up our spurs and take to raising *sheep.*"

"Everybody just relax," Eamon assures us. "The whole thing is cake. There's nothing to it."

Yes, patient reader, we have heard that line before. I am going to spare you the details of the chase, the forty man-hour/sixteen boy-hour chase, up and down the mountainsides of coastal California, over fences, through tangled brush and swollen creek, through the gumbo mud of hillside winter pastures, to fail and fail and fail once more. There is only one image worth recording—a picture of a small, very black cow, a dirty white face, and two red-rimmed eyes that peer sullenly from behind a thicket of coyote brush. The eyes, the ears, the top of the head—nothing more really visible. A bovine Kilroy peeking over the barricade from a wary distance of fifty feet. Because that is as close as we ever got. Five men and two boys. A regiment of guile, cunning, and stealth. Humbert simply ran through us, away from us, over us, and around us. We never laid a glove on him. The little Holstein, As Is, gave up without a struggle. The vet did his job, and As Is was back grazing on thistles before the sun was warm. But not Humbert. Humbert was not interested. All day long Humbert was not interested.

About five o'clock we straggle out of the canyon and back up to the house. The vet, who has come back to see if we have had any luck, shakes his head. "Only way we're going to get him is with a sedative gun. Cost you seventeen dollars more, but from the look of things it might be worth it. Save you boys a lot of wear and tear." What gives this uppity paramedic the idea we're worn and torn? We always lie in the gravel at the close of a lazy day.

"It will have to be next weekend," the vet says. "I'll have to borrow the gun."

"We'll be here," we tell him. "We don't *care* what it costs."

As it turned out, we weren't all there. I developed a cold from running around that day in the damp and drizzle, and by Thursday I was thinking of asking the

vet to come by *my* house with his sedative gun. I called
Robinson instead, to tell him I wouldn't be able to make
it. His wife answered. "Forrest can't come to the
phone," she said. "He's so stiff in the hams he can't
walk." I called Houston to see if he was going to witness
the great event. "Listen man, I've got poison oak like
you wouldn't *believe*. I think I may wind up sterile."

"You too," I tell him sadly.

"What?"

"A victim. Humbert's revenge."

"You better believe it," he says. "It's cost me twenty-
five bucks in cortisone shots. Add that to the soaring cost
of homegrown meat."

But Humbert's real revenge comes on Saturday, with
only Eamon and his boys there to testify. The vet makes
his twenty-dollar house call. He brings his seventeen-
dollar sedative gun, and together they go down in the
lower pasture where Hum is peacefully grazing. There is
a little *peekaboo-I-see-you* maneuvering, with H being
careful to keep a clump of greasewood between himself
and the dawn patrol. What he doesn't notice is the vet
sneaking up on him from behind, and before he knows
what has happened this flanker has pulled out his piece
and zapped him in the ass from a distance of fifty feet.
Eamon joins the vet, they wait for Humbert to keel over,
which, after a suitable length of time, he does, and they
rush on his prostrate form. The vet prepares his equipment. A titter runs through the crowd. In the wings a
marching band and a brace of cannon. The tension is eye-
popping as Eamon slowly lifts Humbert's ratty tail. The
high priest, knife glittering, sinks slowly to his knees . . .

"Mr. Barrett," the vet says, a testy tone to his voice,
"this critter's already been cut. You already *got* a steer."

The ending? There isn't any. But for those organic types considering the virtue of steroid-free beef, the *As Is Cattlemen's Association* offers the following statistics.

Cost of cow:	$287.38
Feed for cow:	$224.00
Vet fees/cow:	$ 77.00
Vet fees/cowboys:	$ 97.33
Slaughtering/butchering:	$135.00
Fines/penalties/repairs:	$103.82
Wages (minimum):	$479.15

It works out to only about four dollars per pound for meat, and you get a story to tell, you cure your supermarket schizophrenia, you get lots of exercise. Living off the land is fun and easy. There's nothing to it. Nothing at all.

Stalking the Wild Boar

It is late in the afternoon. We are sprawled around Eamon Barrett's baronial kitchen, toasting our backsides next to the fire and watching a cold California rain sweep across the ridge and into the canyon below the house. It is mid-December. Christmas is approaching, and the kids are off in the living room trimming a tree under the direction of their mothers, while the male members of this gathering taste their way through a bottle of Leoville Lascases, 2nd cru, 1966, and gloomily regard a heavy overcast driven in off the sea by the south wind. The lower draws of the coast range mountains fill with the storm;

outriding fingers of mist seep up the canyons to meet the leaden sky that has settled into the pine and redwood forests of the higher country.

An inactive day. We are restless. Our host's dog, a scrofulous anthology of respiratory ailments, matted hair, and ill temper, comes into the room and peers through the thicket on his face at Ron Dunton's discarded boots, decides they are probably not edible, and collapses in an aromatic pile by the door. "Why don't you do that animal a favor and shoot it," someone remarks to Eamon.

Eamon, his feet propped on the window sill and his index finger drumming idly against his front teeth, looks fondly at his pet. "I did," he says. "It didn't take."

It starts raining harder, the wind gusting from thirty to forty knots and blowing great holes in the cloud cover below us. I can see the floor of the canyon, periodically, and partway up the side toward the opposite ridge. Wisps of fog snag in the coyote brush and hang there for a moment, flapping.

Dunton gets up, pads to the window in his stocking feet and stands looking out at the storm. "I think we're in for a hell of a winter," he remarks. "I think it's going to be long and cold and wet."

"You can kiss my cabbages goodbye," Eamon says. "I knew I should have planted earlier."

Ron sucks air through his teeth. "You and Stegner ought to slaughter a couple of those scrawny steers of yours and forget the veggies until spring. It's going to be too cold even for a winter garden." He scratches the small of his back and inspects a hole in his sweat sock. "But if things get too tough on you boys I've got a compost heap full of rotten zucchini you can have cheap."

"I'll trade you for that fine bird dog there," Eamon says.

"If things keep on the way they are," I tell Eamon, "I'll fight you for them. The property taxes on my place just went up, the IRS is auditing my returns for the last three years, my daughter needs braces. Her teeth are so crooked if we don't get her to the orthodontist soon we're going to have to put her to sleep."

"Well, you've got to keep the faith," Eamon says. "The land will provide."

"Like it did in Bangladesh?" I tell him. "What the land provides me is aphids, cutworms, sow bugs, leaf miners, earwigs, nematodes, red spiders, and root maggots. All I can eat. And Swiss chard, which is the only thing a gopher won't."

Just before dark, as my wife is making noises from the other room about the lateness of the hour, I pace one more time to the window for a last look at the dingy weather. There is, remarkably, some breakup, and it looks as if it might possibly clear. The canyon is no longer socked in; I can see up toward its northern end where the As Is Cattle Company herd (both of whom were recently impounded for breaking through the fence and running loose on the public roads) are grazing contentedly on stubble and mud. But what catches my eye immediately thereafter is more interesting: four or five hulking animals down the slope some two hundred yards and partially obscured by clumps of poison oak. They seem to be . . . rooting.

"Eamon," I say. "When did you get pigs?"

"No pigs."

"So what is that down there?"

He comes to the window, Ron following, and we stand watching whatever it is for a few moments, until one moves out into a clearing—not more than a dark shadow really, about the size of a large dog: the Hound of the Baskervilles, let us say—and Eamon mutters, "I'll be damned. I believe that is pigs."

"Boar," Ron says. "Wild boar."

"Come on."

Is it possible? We look again, trying to fix their shape in the failing light. "Russian blue, by God. You see how slab-sided they are," Ron says, "with a long sloped back and extended snout?" I peer into the gathering dark and see that he is right, incredibly; they are big and black and hairy, and their tusks gleam dully as they move slowly away from us toward the bottom of the canyon. "There is a fellow in Monterey who raises Russian blue for sport hunting," Ron says. "People pay a big fee. But the strays are fair game, I'd say." Collective grins all around. Oh Eamon, you were right again. The land shall indeed provide.

Sus scrofa. Cloven-hoofed mammal of the family *Suidae.* Once common in the forests of Europe and favorite game of the quality. First imported into this country around 1893 by a man named Austin Corbin, who released fifty boar on his land in New Hampshire, whence they spread themselves around New England. We pass this information around the dinner table as we sit down to eat the Barrett's dinner. Keen of sight, excellent hearing, grow to four hundred pounds. No dear, I'm not embarrassed about staying, even though I wasn't exactly invited.

A boar, I assure Eamon's youngest son, Perry, has the same impulses and instincts as an all-conference linebacker blitzing a quarterback—a metaphor that intrudes itself when I privately consider that the closest I have ever been to a razorback is the front end of a TV set during a Saturday afternoon football game. Ron, however, knows the beast firsthand. When he was a kid, he tells us, his father and uncle hunted them in the Adirondacks, and he knows a couple of good ol' boys down in the Ozarks who track them with special hounds. The score over a season, he says, reads something like hogs 21, dogs 11. Which leads us, of course, into an extended debate over the virtues of various breeds in the hunting of big game—redbone, bluetick, black-and-tan.

Aaron Barrett grows tired of the sporting club prattle. "I'd just like to know when you guys are going to quit jawing and get after these critters."

"Well, now, your boar is mostly a nocturnal feeder," Ron cautions, "though you'll find him around in the early morning too. I think our best bet is about an hour or so before sunup when there is enough light to see but we don't run the risk of becoming the hunted."

"They wouldn't eat you," says Doubting Aaron.

"Not you anyway," Perry tells him. "Nothing could eat *that* much."

Eamon goes to his closet and drags out an old M-1, heavy as a truck axle and slightly rusty, but possibly in working order. He slides the bolt and snaps the trigger.

"You have cartridges for that blunderbuss?"

"With this you don't need cartridges. You corner your prey and throw rocks at it until it attacks you. Then you club it to death."

"I see. That way you run no risk of spoiling your meat, right? Whereas if you actually *shot* anything with it you would have you some ticks and hair and a hole, but not a lot else."

"PIG MEAT," Eamon says. "Think about it, gentlemen.

The hams and the bacons, the ribs and loins. A veritable mountain of sweet, fat pork—sausages, chops. I *told* you something would turn up."

"Pickled pigs' feet," Perry shouts, infected by his father's enthusiasm. "Liver and lights, head cheese . . ."

"Chitlins and menudo," yells gourmet Aaron.

Eamon regards them with a certain distate. "I'm saddened to see you slaver at the prospect of carrion, boys," he says. "We're not buzzards here, you know."

It remains only to set an hour to meet. Dunton will bring me a gun, he says, since I own nothing more formidable than a .22. Ron's wife, Terri, will join us, though my wife and Wendy Barrett want no part of the proceedings. They plan a trip to San Francisco to see a Bufano exhibit or the Brundage collection at the DeYoung, or to take tea in the gardens at Golden Gate Park. Thin blood. Frail stock. It's not clear they intend to return.

In the morning there is just the faintest line of slate-pale light above the Salinas Valley when I leave the town of Santa Cruz and turn east into the foothills. Tule fog floats over the macadam, but the sky is full of stars, and in the rearview mirror I can see a half-moon hanging over the rim of the Pacific. The road begins to climb, ducks into a tunnel of thick vegetation, dark and shapeless as the night, emerges again at the top of the ridge that leads to Eamon's house. Lights are burning in the kitchen when I drive up, and I am the last to arrive. Ron and Terri are drinking coffee. The kids are breakfasting on sweet rolls and Koogle—some revolting homogenization of peanut butter and chocolate. Ron pours a slug of brandy in a cup and adds instant Sanka. "I thought I had another rifle," he says, handing me the hot water, "but I must have lent it

to Terri's brother. I brought you this handgun instead."
He lays the butt of an ugly little pistol in my hand, and I
read Sentinel Mark III stamped into its business end. It is
a .375 magnum with a two-and-a-half-inch barrel and
combat handles, and it is loaded with .270-gram, soft-
point bullets that look as if they could stop a dump truck.
"It might be a little heavy-duty," he admits, "but if we get
any boar charging in on us, you'll be glad you have it."
My only consolation is that I don't think that I'm going
to need it, what with Eamon's M-1 and Ron's Harrington
& Richardson carbine, 30-06, with a Mannlicher stock
and mounted with a 4X Imperial.

"Well," Terri says, putting down her cup, "looks like we
might as well saddle up."

At the end of the ridge we split into two groups. Eamon takes his boys and crosses the canyon, signals us
from the other side, and we work our way in tandem,
descending slowly toward the creek at the edge of the
property. No sign of the boar. We smoke a cigarette and
consider their absence, decide that they have probably
moved onto the adjoining land and that we'll likely find
them along the bottom where a stock road runs through
a long narrow gully and out into an open meadow. It is
still very dark in the canyon, and I am beginning to imagine a malevolent *Sus scrofa* out there in the brush, sharp-
ening his razor tusks on a slab of granite and waiting
impatiently for breakfast to blunder into his space. "Why
don't I go back to the house and drive the truck down this
road," I suggest. "You guys can herd the pigs this way.
When they get into the narrows I'll run over them."

"Fan out the way we were before," Ron orders. "We'll
try the same pattern. Eamon, you give us a signal when
you get up the hill."

It is more than a mile before we see them. As I traverse the slope and climb over a fence with a *No Trespassing* sign on it, I see four shapes beneath the great twisted branches of an oak, rooting in the leaf mold for acorns, tearing up the ground, and moving slowly east toward the dawn. "There they are," Ron hisses, and we hunker down in the brush and freeze. In the shadow of the tree, and from a distance of seventy yards, it is impossible to see more than the dark form of what resembles a hog—or a sheep or a pony or a baby gorilla, depending on what you are expecting in the first place. The light is still weak, and we decide to move closer to get a better shot, though I have made up my mind to leave the Mark III in its holster unless I am attacked. I would rather forgo the debatable pleasure of the kill than blow off my foot.

We move cautiously around the edge of a thicket of poison oak and come out slightly on top of the clearing, to the left of our prey, and twenty or thirty yards closer. A bit below us is a good stand of low coyote brush, and on hands and knees, one at a time, we stealthily move toward it—Terri first, me, then Ron. Three of the boar are back in the tall grass beyond the oak, but one stands in full view, broadside, chewing mindlessly and staring in our direction—right at our bush, as a matter of fact. He does not seem as large, somehow, as I remember him, and with morning light beginning to filter into the valley, not as black either.

"Ron," Terri whispers, "you sure that's a boar?"

Ron is cautiously retracting the bolt on his carbine, injecting a cartridge into its chamber.

"Ron, what are those white spots on its belly?"

He eases the bolt home. "Sow," he whispers. "The big ones are in the grass." To me he says, "See if you can work your way up the canyon a bit. Keep your eye peeled for the others, and if they come busting out when I shoot, open up. And for Christ's sake, be quiet. They locate us, and they're gone."

On my belly I start worming my way toward a patch of scrub oak, keeping my eye on that solitary pig, hoping that the wind won't blow my scent toward her and give me away. Ten yards. Twenty. My pants are soaked with dew, and my glasses keep fogging up. A red-tailed hawk soars over the ridge, hunting, and a rabbit I have not seen scampers for cover. Then I am behind the scrub and skulking my way around its far edge to where I can see the bottom of the canyon again.

All of a sudden, from the opposite slope and behind me, I hear . . . the sweet sound of children's voices. Yelling, crashing through the brush, floundering about. *"Hey, Dad, there's one, Dad, right there you turkey."* And the next thing I know there are a number of explosions. A lot of dirt flies around that one lonely sow, who stands dumbfounded, no doubt wondering what on earth is happening here, anyway? World War III? Then more shots, and she rears on her hind legs, does an *entrechat quatre,* a *plié* and buys the farm. For a moment all is quiet, even the boys. Then, from out of the brush, her three companions burst in a maddened charge, grunting, obviously confused, but crazed killers nevertheless, looking for somebody to run down and spear. Our assault force drops two of them in their tracks, and the fourth . . . well, the fourth just tucks his kinky tail between his fat little hams and shags up the creek.

From behind our respective covers we come, the hunters, striding down the hill into the clearing, stopping, approaching warily, guns at the ready in case one of these awesome brutes is only wounded and still able to launch an attack. It is a needless precaution. The enemy has been rendered inoperative.

"Hey Eamon," Perry says, standing over what now appears to be a rather small pile of pig. "Why do they have tags in their ears?"

Later that afternoon, after a call to the county brand inspector to find out who owned the swine "found grazing on the Barrett property," and after a hit or two on the bottle of Pinch Eamon bought his boss for Christmas but hasn't wrapped yet, three of us drive up the gulch road to the Gaudini Ranch and have a little talk with the foreman in charge. He is very understanding. He himself once mistook a Holstein for a six-point buck up there in his native state of Oregon, and he can readily see how one might confuse four Poland China piglets for a gaggle of wild boar, given bad enough light and great enough distance. "You boys is what they might call victims of hog fever," he opines. We scuff our toes in the dirt and squint at the sky, wondering if it's going to rain. "But I reckon no real damage been done—except to those pigs, heh heh— so long as you're willing to make it up to Mr. Gaudini."

"Of course," we say. "What would you think fair?"

"Oh, well, I'd say about a hundred and fifty bucks would make us square."

"Very decent of you."

"Per pig," he says.

"Per pig?"

"That'd help calm Mr. Gaudini down. I told him there weren't any point calling the county on this. They'd just fine your butts *and* take your meat. Now that it's did, you might as well enjoy it."

"Yes sir," we say. "Can you take a check?"

My wife finds little in all this that amuses her. "You're a regular Euell Gibbons," she says at the supper table. "If you keep this up we'll *all* be eating pine trees pretty soon. If we had the money you've paid in fines over the last year we could dine out four nights a week."

"No we couldn't," I say. "Not even at the Sizzler."

She shovels an omelette onto my plate and opens the cottage cheese. "Undersized abalone, illegal clamming, steelhead fishing without a license, transporting steers in an unsafe vehicle, impounding fees every time your chickens get loose and wipe out the Reeses' garden. Now you're a *rustler* or something. And I wasn't thinking about the Sizzler."

"It's your favorite restaurant."

She pours me a glass of milk. "Living off the fat of the land, my foot. It's a good thing you weren't born a hundred years ago or they'd hang every last one of you."

"Shut up and pass the Bac-o-Bits," I sigh. "I never could stand eggs without side meat."

Wynken, Blynken, and Cod

It strikes me, as I am dining one evening with Jack and Corda Zajac, and we begin to dissect this terrific lingcod Corda has stuffed and baked, that the whole answer to the problem of trying to live off the land is not to. Enough of the impulse to restore economic balance through backyard farming. The evidence is in. As all my earnest attempts at self-sufficiency demonstrate, there is a clear and simple reason why the feedlot and the supermarket thrive. You can't make it in the natural food business, because the people in the unnatural food business do it cheaper and faster, and when they suffer a loss, it's their loss, not yours. One skunk in the henhouse can put you out of the poultry game—fast.

But, I observe, as I wash down another flaky morsel of cod with a soupçon of cold Chablis, to go down to the sea in ships is a different kettle of fish. Your basic fish is not only abundant in the wild, it is tasty, better for you than anything else you can eat, and now too expensive to buy off the rack. Tracking the noble Pisces may just be the answer to easy living. You don't have to feed it, water it, spray it, mulch it, put straw in its bed, muck around in its dung. All you need is a ten-cent hook, a sinker, a piece of string, and some bait. It astounds me, as I accept thirds, that for all the years I've logged on the Pacific coast it has never occurred to me that for a dime I can just walk out there on the water and reap nature's bounty—get my exercise, my rest and relaxation, fill the freezer, throw fabulous dinner parties, be the envy of all my friends, the first on my block—all free, gratis. Of course, if one had a small craft with a motor on it, one could go after the big stuff. Salmon. Tuna. Albacore.

"Would you by any chance have an interest in going shares on a fishing boat?" I ask Jack. I do not dignify with so much as a glance my wife's groan.

I should point out that Jack is a *real* fisherman: the kind who ties his own flies, wades around up to his bum in freezing rivers, keeps his rods in metal tubes; the kind who looks at a stretch of water and reads its bottom from the riffles; the kind you see featured in your monthly copy of *Field & Stream*. Some people know him as one of America's most respected sculptors, but the distinction is a quibble. Aesthetic passion motivates Jack. His hand-tied Muddler Minnows belong in the Lytton Collection along with his impaled goats. My question is obviously rhetorical. Of course he's interested in going shares on a fishing boat. A fishing boat is the missing element in the drama of his life. That he should live but a stone's throw from the shores of the Pacific, that he should stand but five hundred yards from the lighthouse banks and lack the simple machinery to get out and whale into the midst of a perpetual cod frenzy, saddens him profoundly. We discuss the relative merits of the V and the planning hull, the Johnson and the Evinrude, the electric and the hydraulic gurdy.

I should also mention what while Jack may be the quintessential fisherman, he knows little about boats and cares not a fig for the mystery of the two-cycle engine. This is where I come in. I don't know my reel from my creel, as usual, but I've been a sea dog all my life. I took third place in the Greensboro, Vermont Sunfish regatta in 1964. Moreover, I owned a beat-up Harley-Davidson when I was seventeen, and as I recall it had a two-cycle engine just like an outboard. Or was it two cylinders? Whatever.

"I'll take care of technology," I say. "You just lead us to the fish."

"What about a Boston Whaler?" Jack says. "I hear they're fantastic."

"Yeah, but bloody expensive," I tell him. "Listen, I heard about a converted dory this guy is selling over in Aptos. Why don't I just snoop around a little and see what I come up with?"

I confess to a certain impatience when shopping.

When I want something I want it because I need it because I have to have it *right now*. So it was a good thing it was love at first sight between me and *la petite Madeleine*. Sturdy craft, *la petite*. Eighteen feet long, with the flared bow of the Oregon dory, decked over just forward amidships, with a tiny cabin poking up there like the wheelhouse of a Monterey purse seiner, portholes and all. Aft of the cabin a cockpit with an outrageously nautical wheel, controls for the engine, a tach and a speedometer, and behind that an open space for gurdy stanchions, fish box, and fisherman. Maybe even two fishermen.

And none of your plastic stinkpot, *la petite Madeleine*. All wood, painted workboat grey, trimmed in white, and, by gum, you can just tell by looking at her that she's made for heavy seas, for plowing through the surge with that flared bow, throwing the spray clear, churning green water white in her foaming wake . . .

The only thing of some small concern is a rather ratty-looking 35-horse Johnson outboard hanging off her stern. A real antique. But no big deal. Those two-cycles run forever.

The captain of this fantasy assures me that she is as sound as the day she was launched. Her engine has never so much as hiccuped, and she'll run four and a half hours on a tank of fuel. She draws about two feet, makes an easy eight knots. She comes complete with anchor, bilge pump, compass, hand gurdies, motor, trailer, and lots of luck to you, my friend. I check out the trailer, which seems to have been remodeled with chunks of four-by-four and long strips of electrical tape, and note with satisfaction that there is good tread on the tires. "I'll talk to my partner," I tell the captain. "I'll give you a call."

You can tell that Jack is overwhelmed when he sees

la petite for the first time. There are tears in his eyes. "Jesus Christ, it's a . . . it's a . . . *toy*. A toy boat. You're not . . . I mean you can't . . . be serious."

"Well," I say, a little hurt, "it was just an idea. Just shopping around."

"Where do the people go?"

"I think there's room for four. Maybe three. As the owner points out, you can stow all your gear in the cabin. Out of the way. Very handy."

Jack walks around to the other side, exploding into periodic guffaws. "I'll be *damned!*" he says, about every fifteen seconds. Then he walks off and studies her from a distance, like a piece of sculpture or a *tsaftig* young model. "It is . . . cute," he admits.

Taking heart, I point out the virtues of the dory hull, how dry in lumpy seas, how commodious, actually, if not overpopulated. "See that deck space between the cockpit and gunwales? That's where you lay out your rods, baited hooks, gaff, net. Pretty slick, what?"

"The sonofabitch must weigh a ton," Jack says. "How would we get it in the water?"

"She has a slip down in the harbor," I inform him, playing my trump card. "It's part of the deal."

That turns him around. A slip in Santa Cruz is worth its volume in Dom Perignon. People wait up to seven years for a slip. The prospect of stepping aboard, firing up the engine, and chugging out to sea so appeals to Jack, when he considers the hassle of launching (at four bucks a pop) from the public ramp, that he just about capitulates.

"How much is a slip?"

"Dollar and a half a foot per month."

"Pretty steep."

"Ah, but I have that all figured out, you see. Way out in front of you. What we do is we *sell* the fish we don't need for ourselves down at the wharf for two bits a pound. I'm told there are guys that come in after a day at Seven Mile Reef with three, four hundred *pounds* of rockfish, and it doesn't take an accountant to figure out we don't have to do a lot of business to pay all our expenses and a few bar bills to boot."

"I'll be damned," Jack says. He circles the *Madeleine* a few more times. "It might be ... amusing, you know?"

I pull my lip, furrow my brow in thought. Let us not appear to act importunately. Or to have made up our minds prior to sober consideration. "Absolutely. I don't see how we can go wrong. Especially considering the fact that we'll have this bucket paid off in three months."

"Why don't we just sleep on it one night," Jack says.

So we sleep on it. And the next day we each write a check for half a boat. And then I go down to the Harbor Marina and buy myself one of those snazzy caps you see up there on the flying bridge of tuna boats—the one with the black bill and the baby-blue top and the insignia with the two crossed anchors embossed in gold.

So Laurel and Hardy go fishing. And after they rent their boat and row a mile or two out, Hardy manages to snag a dogfish which he reels in and lands in Laurel's lap. Receives a box on the ear. Laurel bends over and chalks an X on the bottom of the boat. "What on earth is that for, Stanley?" "Why, so the next time we come fishing we'll know where the good spot is, Oliver." Receives a blip on the noodle. "Stupid! How do you know we'll get the same boat the next time?"

The co-captains of *la petite Madeleine* accommodate no such foolishness. It's strictly yo-ho-heave-ho on the *Madeleine*. In a little over three and a half hours their fish box holds six lingcod of an average weight of about ten pounds, plus a large assortment of other bottom fish, and they are headed back to the safety of the harbor. Captain Jack marvels at the richness of the Pacific. By contrast, he observes, the Mediterranean is a dead sea. Captain Page whistles tunelessly as he steers for the distant jetty. There'll be no shufflin' along the widow's walk today.

Actually Captain Page's spirits are now quite high. The mild depression and first phase of migraine that threatened earlier this morning (as he wrote out a staggering check to the bait shop for fishing equipment he'd forgotten he didn't own any of) have been completely dispelled. Now that he's killed something he feels a lot better. A one-time expense, that seventy-five bucks for rod, reel, weights, line, cod rigs, bait, and Rolaids. Well . . . almost. He's still a bit alarmed by the rapid rate at which those cod rigs and weights seem to snag down there in the rocks at ten fathoms, and by the apparent impossibility of getting them loose except by busting them off the line. Metaphorically speaking, every time he busts his line (about once every twenty minutes) he stands up and throws two bucks into the ocean. Captain Jack assures him that the skills will soon be acquired and the losses cut to a pittance.

Fuel consumption is something else again. Laurel

calls Hardy's attention to the fact that their trusty outboard has sucked up nearly all of its allotted six gallons
in the four hours they have been out. This is as advertised, to be sure, but puzzling, as they have spent nearly
three of those hours drifting. Perhaps a tune-up is in
order, they tell each other. Be a sour note to run out of
gas just as they're trying to gun it through the surf break
that occurs in the harbor mouth every winter. Could
lose the boat that way, Paco. "*Si,*" Paco says. "Better get
a tune-up."

The old Seahorse confirms this diagnosis by suddenly going into epileptic seizure, swallowing its
tongue, farting great clouds of oily smoke, rattling
through one final, violent shudder, and dying. "Now
what?" Captain Jack says.

Now what indeed? Plugs? Points? Carburetor? They
are low on gas, but not out. Who understands the two-
cycle engine here? Is there a mechanic in the audience?
They stare at the quisling for a few minutes, pondering
the steam rising from its propeller shaft; then, for lack
of a better idea, begin to dismantle it. Captain Page tries
to take off the clutch and fuel lines that run forward to
the controls so that he can then unsnap the cover
latches and get into the heart of the matter, but he finds
it not so easy to work on a hot engine while hanging
off the end of a boat that rocks and pitches and threat-
ens to broach with each passing swell. And by this time
they have drifted considerably closer to the shore. "Hey,
Paco, the rocks," Captain Jack says. "You better get
something happening with that motor pretty quick."

Captain Page finally gets the lines free, only to discover that the snaps holding the hinged sections of the
engine cover are so corroded by salt that they won't

budge. "I need something to pry this with," he yells, and Captain Jack hunts around in the cabin until he comes up with the boathook, the end of which is sharp enough to work into the curve of the snaps. Captain Page jimmies open the left side; the right is more stubborn. Stubborn starboard. Red right returning. Captain P works his pry into the clamp. The *Madeleine* ascends gracefully to the top of an enormous swell, flops over the top, and tips down into the trough just as he puts his back into it, heaving from the knees like a weight lifter demonstrating the clean and jerk. The clamp snaps off with a *whizzzingggg* and Captain P teeters frantically on the transom, grappling with his hook for something, anything, to save him from a bath. He snags the steering pulley, does a roadrunner number off the bosom of the next wave, regains his balance, and falls into the cockpit just in time to watch the engine cover rattle over the stern and sink like a stone beneath the waves. "Sheeeeit," says Captain Jack. "Now what?"

The sound of surf pounding against the wall of the jetty some three hundred yards away just cannot be ignored. But no cause for alarm. Not yet. As any seasoned tar knows, there are various support systems that come into play in the event of an emergency. Captain Page doesn't have that insignia pasted on his cap for *nothing*. Get the anchor, quick. "CHRIST JESUS ALMIGHTY, WE'RE ALMOST ON THE ROCKS, JACK," he calmly orders, and Captain Jack, banging his head and jamming his shoulders in the doorway of that goddamn, dinky, Lilliputian, Pop-Warner league cabin, eventually emerges with a hunk of rusty old iron that would be serviceable enough except that it has no line attached to it. He drops it on the deck and regards it as if it's something he stepped in. "We fucked up, big time," he says.

The main thing is to stay cool. Nobody panic. Take your seats, please. Should it become necessary to abandon ship, members of the crew have been trained in evacuation procedures, and you can rest assured that they will evacuate at the slightest hint of danger, so kindly watch where you put your feet. Now, if we can all, on the count of three, begin waving our shirts like lunatics, perhaps some landlubber will take notice . . .

Even as we speak. Avast there, Captain Jack, belay yourself and ready to throw the harbor patrol a line.

"We don't have a line," Jack says. "We left it on the dock."

Nobody expects a shakedown cruise to go off without a hitch. Murphy's Law, which everybody knows states if something *can* screw up, it *will,* does not exempt ships at sea. In fact, Murphy was probably a boat owner. And the owners of *la petite Madeleine* are profoundly convinced that it is a good thing to get the bugs worked out right off the bat rather than to have real trouble someday when they're a long way from shore. Jack goes off to get the anchor rigged with chain and line; I take the outboard down to the repair shop to see about having it tuned. We also need a new motor cover.

The mechanic at Thrash Marina is a nice man, but when he speaks about the nuts and bolts of an outboard engine he speaks in tongues—a shortcoming, it seems, of most technicians. I tell him what's wrong with my Seahorse (based on what it sounded like just before it quit), and after an indulgent pause he tells *me* what's wrong with it. There is no similarity in the diagnoses.

I say plugs and points. He says, "The dogshift is rounded off here so that it won't mesh with the schnazzelphring because the turnsnicket has been grooved over there at the base of the frump. That means your wranger won't penetrate the orifice of the nimble, so your trammelsnag just hangs there at six o'clock all day. You got to replace the dogshift."

I don't want to argue about it. You can pick your nose and you can pick your banjo, but you can't wipe your banjo on your pants. I defer to the expert. "How much will it cost?"

"Oh, I dunno. About a hundred bucks, I'd guess."

"How much is this thing worth in the first place?"

"Oh, I dunno. Not much more than that."

"If I have it fixed, how long would you say it'll last?"

"Oh, I dunno. Maybe a few months, maybe a few years."

"So I might just be throwing good money after bad."

"Might be."

"But you never know."

"You never know."

"I see. Well, that's very helpful, but let me put it to you another way. If this were your engine, what would you do with it?"

"Well, it wouldn't cost *me* a hundred bucks to fix. I'm the fixer."

"Is there anything else that could be haywire beside the dogshit?"

"Dogshift."

"Right."

"Dunno. Could be. But you can't tell till you fix the jdogshift."

"How much does a new motor cost? One like this."

"Around eleven hundred, with the tank."

"Fix the dogshift."

"You're the boss."

"I wish that were so."

My day has not ended. When I get home I suddenly realize that I have between thirty and forty pounds of fish to clean—rockfish, yet, all full of spines and pricklers and razor-sharp teeth. When I'm finished I have so many holes in me I look like Saint Sebastian, but my kids come out to view the catch and restore my faith in the whole enterprise.

"Yuk," says my daughter.

"That's a lot of codfish. I'm not all that into codfish," says my wife.

"I won't eat that," says my son.

The forecast is for clear skies and gentle winds up to fifteen knots. The high-pressure area holding winter storms off the California coast remains in place, and we have temperatures ranging up to seventy degrees. Terrific. The only trouble is that huge swells make bottom fishing hopeless, and by noon we decide to give it up. Mustn't get discouraged. It's only our second time out, and we'll learn. Our engine runs fine now, and we have a nice new forty-dollar anchor rope and chain. We even have flares so we won't have to make a spectacle of ourselves waving dirty T-shirts around. The only thing we haven't counted on is the four-to-six-foot breakers that are smashing right across the mouth of the harbor. There are kids *surfing* in the harbor. "Just how are we supposed to get through that?" Jack says, surveying the scene from our bow.

"It's all in the timing," I tell him. "What you have to

do is wait for the set to go through; then you have about a minute before the next one comes and you just put the boots to her and scoot right in. Nothing to it. All in the timing."

We circle just outside the mouth, watching the swells, counting—four, five, six—until the sea flattens out behind the seventh wave—*Now! Go for it*—and we put the "boots" to her; our bow surges up out of the sea like Moby Dick about to ram the *Pequod,* the engine rattles like a cement truck full of marbles and churns a veritable highway of white water in our wake—hang on to your hats, boys, we're closing. God help the hot dog who gets in our way. I glance at our speedometer, amazed to see it fixed at *five miles an hour,* rigid, as if it's broken or something; Christ's mother, at this speed we'll be run over by every single wave in the set we're supposed to be scooting in in front of, we'll be creamed . . .

The first wave breaks about ten feet behind us, picking our stern up just high enough for the second to roll in underneath and keep us out there on the curl, hanging ten, as it were, with our prop out of the water and zero steerage, a perfect setup for number three to knock us sideways so that we roll and broach under number four. Whoopee! There goes my forty-dollar rod and reel. There goes the fish box . . . look out, here it comes back, goddamn, it, where's my hat? Five, six, and seven commit unspeakable acts on *Madeleine's* backside, Eight, nine, ten—is there no end to this atrocity?

There is. Somehow we come through upright, ungrounded, only partially swamped, and when the turbulence ceases there we are, floating sublimely up the harbor to the cheers, catcalls, and howls of derision from the lunch crowd at the Crow's Nest Restaurant immediately to our left. Which should be our right. It seems we've gotten turned around and are proceeding homeward stern first.

The harbor patrol isn't howling. The harbor patrol doesn't care if we come home lashed to the spars. What they want to know is why we haven't paid the bill on our end-tie. Twenty-three days at two-fifty a day, and unless we have a permanent slip lined up, which is impossible because there aren't any, we'd better make plans for the immediate removal of our vessel. The time limit on an end-tie is two weeks. Stop by the office anytime, gentlemen, and settle up.

"End-tie? I thought the guy we bought this can from said it had a slip," Jack says.

"Well, he said it was *in* a slip. Perhaps I gave a more liberal interpretation . . ."

Jack empties the water out of his shoes and peels off his socks. His toes, marinated for the last three hours in oily bilge, look like old bait. I discover my hat floating in the motor well with a half-dozen soggy squid. "I guess we have to pull it out," I say. "Anyway, by salmon season next month we can lease a slip because I hear a lot of these bigger boats take off for five, six months." I put hat on with the bill pointing backward. "We might as well wait for salmon season ourselves. They've got to have that harbor mouth dredged by then."

"If we're going to do it," Jack says, "we better do it right now, because tomorrow I have to go to Los Angeles for a week."

Back at the house, an inspection of the trailer reveals some missing parts overlooked at the time of purchase—specifically, the parts you need to attach it to whatever you intend to haul it with. Grand Auto provides these items for eleven dollars and ninety-nine cents. A welder in their tire shop attaches them in a record-breaking hour and a half (at twenty bucks an hour), and it occurs to me suddenly that the cost of those jolly lingcod I was so proud of the other day has now risen to approximately two hundred and thirty dollars apiece. And we still owe fifty-seven bucks for the end-tie. I wonder what they do if you won't pay?

We get the trailer together by three o'clock and are back down at the harbor ready to float the *Madeleine* on and take her home. I drop Jack at the end-tie and drive back to the outer harbor to the launching ramp. Disappointing, all this. Not quite as planned back there at the beginning, but surely there are limits to the suffering one must endure. Does no honorable impulse *ever* go unpunished? I mean, all we wanted to do was provide for the family. We weren't greedy.

When I see Jack putting down the channel I back the truck down the ramp and ease the trailer into the water. With any luck he can coast her right on. If he cuts the engine and figures the drift just right, he can slip the bow in between the stanchions, I'll clip the winch on the rings, and we'll snub her down into her cradle. Be home by cocktails. Easy there, Jack, back off now, throw her in reverse and a touch of throttle. More throttle. *More throttle, Jack, YOU'RE GONNA RAM THE DOCK* ... no, belay that, it's perfect. He's done it perfectly. Grease her on in there now. Four-point landing. Could use you on one of those Liberian tankers, Jack. What a helms ...

Kerwhompscriiiitchhthunk! My hat falls off. The trailer bucks and moves sideways five feet and the truck shudders, slides back till its hubs are under water. I clamber out of the cab, dash into the channel to join Jack, who is up to his waist in the surge, grappling for the bowline of *la petite* pain-in-the-ass *Madeleine,* and hurling abuse at her sullen hulk. *"Pig. Toad-boat!"*

"What happened?" I gargle. "You were right on the mark."

"Yeah, but four feet too deep. To get this bastard on the trailer we'll have to back the truck into the middle of the channel. *Scum-sucking dungheap. Swine. Whore.*"

"How is this possible? Why us?"

Jack's face is so long that when he gets home tonight he's going to have to unbutton his shirt to eat his dinner. "I've had it. I'm taking this sucker back to the end-tie. I don't care if they impound it, or burn it at the dock."

I climb wearily back into the truck and watch him chug out into the main channel. He's right, of course. Enough is enough. The bounty of the sea is going the way of the fat of the land. I quit. I give up. I'm going back to my desk. A schmuck with an Underwood shall always be a schmuck with an Underwood. Nothing more. What we all need now is extended shore leave.

"So like I was talking to Mr. Zajac," the kid at my front door says, "and he was telling me how terrific the fishing is on Monterey Bay, and he said you guys might consider an offer on your boat. You know, if it was good enough to get you into a bigger one."

I inspect this gull, this mark, this exemplum of P. T. Barnum's observation on the birth of the sucker, and I find him without defect. He is young, long-haired, bright-eyed, and looks like the kind of sanguine zealot one finds in natural food stores buying seeds and nuts. He wears waffle-stompers, ski socks that come halfway up his calf, blue hiking shorts from REI, and a Patagonia jacket. A walking, biorhythmic dithyramb. He has a Indo-rag tied around his blond Afro, and is probably an environmental studies major.

"By all means. Come on out back and I'll show her to you."

The kid inspects the *Madeleine,* talking nonstop in a language that seems related to English but syntactically modeled on Croatian. The gist of his patter I seem to understand. He shares a house with two gentlemen of his own age and persuasion. They have arrived at the conclusion that "the mass commodity exchange has disenfranchised the people and foreclosed on the rights of self-determination and procurement," and they have determined to do something about it "life-stylewise." They grow organic veggies. They have chickens. They wish to expand their protein source and try fishing.

"My boy," I tell him, "you and your friends are very shrewd. You're right on the cutting edge. See, most people never observe. Most people live right here on the brink of one of the richest upwellings in the Pacific and never think to put it to their own use. They look out across Monterey Bay and all they see is a view. You see it as nature's feedlot. You . . ."

"You really catch enough to cover your investment?"

"Son, are you into salmon? Are you into tuna, yellowtail, bonito, albacore, halibut, sole? Can you relate to four hundred pounds of rockfish in a single day's outing?"

"*Seriously?*"

LIVING OFF THE FAT OF THE LAND

"Honor-bound."

"That's totally awesome."

"Totally awesome. Listen, my boy, I don't want to oversell you on this boat, because I'm not sure I even want to part with it. I love this little boat. But let me tell you about the last time me and my partner, Jack, went out. Have you ever taken a ten-cent hook, a piece of string, and a little one-pound sinker and dropped it overboard with a hunk of squid on it, and inside two minutes hauled in a twenty-pound lingcod? Well, on this boat here, on *la petite Madeleine* . . ."